T0362924

PUBLISHED BY BOOM BOOKS

www.boombooks.biz

ABOUT THIS SERIES

.... But after that, I realised that I knew very little about these parents of mine. They had been born about the start of the Twentieth Century, and they died in 1970 and 1980. For their last 50 years, I was old enough to speak with a bit of sense.

I could have talked to them a lot about their lives. I could have found out about the times they lived in. But I did not. I know almost nothing about them really. Their courtship? Working in the pits? The Lock-out in the Depression? Losing their second child? Being dusted as a miner? The shootings at Rothbury? My uncles killed in the War? Love on the dole? There were hundreds, thousands of questions that I would now like to ask them. But, alas, I can't. It's too late.

Thus, prompted by my guilt, I resolved to write these books. They describe happenings that affected people, real people. The whole series is, to coin a modern phrase, designed to push your buttons, to make you remember and wonder at things forgotten.

The books might just let nostalgia see the light of day, so that oldies and youngies will talk about the past and re-discover a heritage otherwise forgotten. Hopefully, they will spark discussions between generations, and foster the asking and answering of questions that should not remain unanswered.

BORN IN 1966?

WHAT ELSE HAPPENED?

RON WILLIAMS

AUSTRALIAN SOCIAL HISTORY

BOOK 28 IN A SERIES OF 35
FROM 1939 to 1973

War Babies Years (1939 to 1945): 7 Titles
Baby Boom Years (1946 to 1960): 15 Titles
Post Boom Years (1961 to 1972): 13 Titles

BOOM, BOOM BABY, BOOM

BORN IN 1966? WHAT ELSE HAPPENED?

Published by Boom Books.
Wickham, NSW, Australia
Web: www.boombooks.biz
Email: email@boombooks.biz

© Ron Williams 2016. This edition 2023

A single chapter or part thereof may be copied and reproduced without permission, provided that the Author, Title, and Web Site are acknowledged.

Creator: Williams, Ron, 1934- author
Title: Born in 1966? : what else happened? / Ron Williams.
ISBN: 9780987543684 (paperback)
Series: Born in series, book 28.
Almanacs, Australian.
Australia--History--Miscellanea--20th century.
Dewey Number: 994.04

Some Letters used in this text may still be in copyright. Every reasonable effort has been made to locate the writers. If any persons or their estates can establish authorship, and want to discuss copyright, please contact the author at email@boombooks.biz

Cover image: National Archives of Australia A1200, L57448, PM Harold Holt welcomes US President Johnson; A1200, L49212, junior football; A12111, 1/1965/4/13, family outing; A1200, L47077, building workers; A7973, INT812/4, vehicles.

CONTENTS

IMPORTANT PEOPLE AND EVENTS

Queen of England	Elizabeth II
Prime Minister of Oz	Robert Menzies
After January, 1966	Harold Holt
Leader of Opposition	Arthur Calwell
Governor General	Lord Casey
The Pope	Paul VI
US President	Lyndon Johnson
PM of Britain (after April)	Harold Wilson

Holder of the Ashes:

1964	Australia 1 - 0
1965-66	Australia 1 - 1
1968	Australia 1 - 1

Melbourne Cup Winners:

1965	Light Fingers
1966	Galillee
1967	Red Handed

Academy Awards, 1966:

Best Actor	Paul Schofield
Best Actress	Elizabeth Taylor
Best Movie	A Man for all Seasons

PREFACE TO THIS SERIES

This book is the 28th in **a series** of books that I have researched and written. It tells a story about a number of important or newsworthy Australia-centric events that happened in 1966. The **series** covers each of the years from 1939 to 1973, for a total of 35Titles.

I developed my interest in writing these books a few years ago at a time when my children entered their teens. My own teens started in 1947, and I tried to remember what had happened to me then. I thought of the big events first, like Saturday afternoon at the pictures, and cricket in the back yard, and the wonderful fun of going to Maitland on the train for school each day. Then I recalled some of the not-so-good things. I was an altar boy, and that meant three or four Masses a week. I might have thought I loved God at that stage, but I really hated his Masses. And the schoolboy bullies, like Greg Favel and the hapless Freddie Bevin. Yet, to compensate for these, there was always the beautiful, black headed, blue-sailor-suited June Brown, who I was allowed to worship from a distance.

I also thought about my parents. Most of the major events that I lived through came to mind readily. But after that, I realised that I really knew very little about these parents of mine. They had been born about the start of the Twentieth Century, and they died in 1970 and 1980. For their last 20 years, I was old enough to speak with a bit of sense. I could have talked to them a lot about their lives. I could have found out about the times they lived in. But I did not. I know almost nothing about them really. Their courtship? Working in the pits? The Lock-out in the Depression? Losing their second child? Being dusted as a miner? The shootings at Rothbury?

My uncles killed in the War? There were hundreds, thousands of questions that I would now like to ask them. But, alas, I can't. It's too late.

Thus, prompted by my guilt, I resolved to write these books. They describe happenings that affected people, real people. In **1966,** there is some coverage of international affairs, but a lot more on social events within Australia. This book, and the whole series is, to coin a modern phrase, designed to push the reader's buttons, to make you remember and wonder at things forgotten. The books might just let nostalgia see the light of day, so that oldies and youngies will talk about the past and re-discover a heritage otherwise forgotten. Hopefully, they will spark discussions between generations, and foster the asking and the answering of questions that should not remain unanswered.

The sources of my material. I was born in 1934, so that I can remember well a great deal of what went on around me from 1939 onwards. But of course, the bulk of this book's material came from research. That meant that I spent many hours in front of a computer reading electronic versions of newspapers, magazines, Hansard, Ministers' Press releases and the like. My task was to sift out, **day-by-day**, those stories and events that would be of interest to the most readers. Then I supplemented these with materials from books, broadcasts, memoirs, biographies, government reports and statistics. And I talked to old-timers, one-on-one, and in organised groups, and to Baby Boomers about their recollections. People with stories to tell came out of the woodwork, and talked no end about the tragic, and funny, and commonplace events that have shaped their lives.

The presentation of each book. For each year covered, the end result is a collection of short Chapters on many of the topics that concerned ordinary people in that year. I think I have covered most of the major issues that people then were interested in. On the other hand, in some cases I have dwelt a little on minor frivolous matters, perhaps to the detriment of more sober considerations. Still, in the long run, this makes the book more readable, and hopefully it will convey adequately the spirit of the times.

Each of the books is mainly Sydney based, but I have been **deliberately national in outlook**, so that readers elsewhere will feel comfortable that I am talking about matters that affected them personally. After all, housing shortages and strikes and juvenile delinquency involved **all** Australians, and other issues, such as problems overseas, had no State component in them. Overall, I expect I can make you wonder, remember, rage and giggle equally, no matter whence you hail.

BACKGROUND TO 1966

I have written 34 books in this series so far. In the first seven of them, 1939 to 1945, I had a feeling of foreboding because I knew full well that they were the War years, and that impossibly difficult times were ahead.

From 1945, and right up till now, I had a happier message. Every year, I could say that things had improved on the previous year, and hopefully that they would be even better next year. In that latter hope, I was in general correct, for most of the population. For one thing, lots of servicemen came home, and were slowly, ever so slowly, taken out of their uniforms. Boys and girls got down to the serious business of courting, and marrying and starting a great baby boom.

Any able-bodied person could find a job, and could enter the great frustrating struggle to get accommodation away from their parents. Gradually, they **did** get their own houses, and cars, and second mortgages, and later TV sets, and of course, Hills Hoists in the backyard. Around them, the nation was doing well too, with only a few wobbles now and then. In the early 1950's, much of the nation actually boomed when the prices of wool and commodities reached record levels as a result of the Korean War.

For the majority of the population, the **pre-war image** was one of the ploughman homeward plodding his weary way. His dwelling was squalid, his wages were meagre, his wife spent her Mondays sweating over the washing, and her Tuesdays over the ironing. The kids were often bare-footed, poorly nourished, and beset with tooth aches, measles, and mumps. Most of them lived in handed-down clothes, and were a blanket short in winter.

From 1945, this melancholy picture had steadily and quickly changed. By the start of 1966, things were entirely different and all the deficiencies that I described above were scarcely on the agenda. For example, new three-bedroom homes in good suburbs were common, some people were getting second cars, schools were adequate, and the price of clothing had fallen beyond anyone's wildest dreams. What I am saying is that materially, every able-bodied person was ever so much better off, and even the infirm and disabled now had something of a security blanket to wrap round themselves.

Importantly, the mood of the population had changed. The dour acceptance of one's unfortunate fate had gone away.

WWI and the Depression left scars and indelible marks, and the mid-1930's were marred by job insecurity and worsening international threat. On top of economic hardship the fear, and then the actuality, of WWII, had haunted the oldies.

But the young men and women who emerged from this War were different. For them, the freedom from the fears of the war, and the restrictions of the war, gave them a realisation that better times were here **now. Many of the old taboos were gone forever.**

At the end of 1965, bikini swimsuits were old hat, some people were no longer standing up for the National Anthem in theatres, many women were not wearing stockings and petticoats, people were allowed to gamble in public, hotels were open till late, many sports were played on Sundays and they charged entrance fees, Hire Purchase had removed the tyranny of the banks in lending, and Rock-and Roll and then the Beatles were disturbing the peace with their performances and riotous audiences.

On a more serious level, **Church attendances were down** and many in the community were feeling emancipated. The fear of God, and the demands of set rituals, were no longer important to them. For them, **God was no longer an angry warder, but had become quite Christian**. Importantly, **blind bigotry**, that had marred the world for centuries, was on the decline. Of course, it still ruined the lives of many, but the thin edge of the wedge was finding cracks.

The white man in Australia was starting to talk about giving the **Aboriginal population** a fair go. **Women** were finding their voices and, as the old model of a man supporting a family of six gave way to everyone for themselves, they were getting closer than before to equal pay for equal work. Importantly, the **contraceptive pill** was now on the scene, and for some women this brought a novel freedom. As I said in my *1965 Conclusion*, "I think women are here to stay."

On the international scene, China and Vietnam were the nation's biggest worry. I won't go into detail here because we will hear a lot of these as the year goes on. Suffice to say that our American friends were convinced that the Chinese Reds were intent on winning military victories in all the nations of South East Asia, then Indonesia, Australia, and their ultimate prize, Tasmania. We were one of America's closest allies, and quite prepared to follow her in most matters. So now that the US was seriously putting fighting troops into Vietnam, we too were sending more and more young men to the slaughter in that country. In 1966, at the start of the year, our Regular Army and our babies in National Service were on their way to the fray, and the nation they left behind was getting more and more anxious.

One overseas factor playing quietly in the background was the demand in many Third World nations for control over their own destinies. This was showing up in riots, battles, uprisings, and overthrows of governments, as well as dubious election results. No continent was spared. Again, we will see more evidence of this as we proceed.

The Sunday afternoon barbeque in a million backyards in Australia was not much disturbed by the latter turmoil. We noted it, tut-tutted about it, and chucked another prawn on the barbie. Mostly, we were a long way from all the heat that these events generated, and we would only get involved when they mattered to us. Which, we all hoped, would be never.

When we sum it up, conditions and attitudes were pretty sanguine. Except for the looming spectre of Vietnam. That might just spoil the barbies. We can only wait and see.

SPECIFIC EVENTS IN 1965

One major event of 1965 was the so-called **Freedom Rides**. These were copies of events in the US, where a number of agitators travelled round the nation, and did what they could to highlight the poor conditions of the coloured people.

In Australia, the agitators were mainly University students, often white, and the focal points were Bogabri and Moree in NSW. The Rides caught the attention of the Press, and that helped to whip up a lot of opinions both for and against the current treatment of Aborigines. This increased the awareness of the plight of this race, and the increased sympathy came to the fore **later in the decade when the Federal Government ran a referendum that granted improved citizenship rights to Aborigines**. At about the same time, the States removed some of their discriminatory legislation and practices. **The Rides softened many attitudes.**

About half-way through the year, **the Beatles got into the news**. There was nothing odd about this, because at the time they featured in most things light and frivolous. This time, they took the limelight because Queen Elizabeth bestowed on all four of them the honour of appointment to Knights of the British Empire (KBE). So, in the Queen's Honours List, there they were, surrounded by life-saving scientists, and doctors and teachers, eminent politicians, and philanthropists. Many Letter-writers to the newspapers questioned whether this was the right way to use the British Honours system. Equally, many people applauded and said bravo. In any case, it is hard to see that the world, or the Empire, or Australia, suffered too much as a result.

Bob Menzies had been Prime Minister for 16 years, and was as comfortable as could be. He controlled the parliamentary votes of his own Liberal Party and also those of Arthur Fadden's Country Party, and he and they had unworried control of the legislation and administration of the nation.

The Opposition was led by Arthur Calwell, who, according to my Dad, had one of the best Labor minds of the 1850's. Whether that was true or not, Calwell was struggling to gain any sort of traction against the Liberals, and was fighting non-stop to control the factions battling within his own Party. About every second election during Menzies' reign, Labor got reasonably close to gaining power, but had never succeeded since the days of Ben Chifley. To jump ahead for a moment, Labor remained out of office until the heady days of the new leader, Gough Whitlam, in the early Seventies.

Menzies was a very persuasive and eloquent speaker. **He used his oratory endlessly to berate the Communists.** This well-organised and passionate group of advocates wanted to see a Communist state replace our easy-going democracy, so that it would be **the state** that allocated all resources, owned all property and took all the profits. The profits would then be shared among the workers. In short, they wanted a Communist state, along the lines of Russia or maybe China.

Within the Australian Communist Party, there were two distinct groups. **Firstly**, there were many who wanted to see the transformation to the Red state brought about by violent revolution. That would mean the overthrow of the government, probably the lopping of heads, and the creation of a bureaucracy that would bring in the ideal state. The key point was that they wanted **a violent revolution** to make the change.

Then there was a **second group**, much more moderate, who wanted the changes, but hoped they could make them in **a non-violent manner**. It was alright with them if they could cripple the economy by strikes, if that weakened the government to the point of collapse. That would make possible the creation of a new socialist state.

The two groups came together uneasily into one Party. It never did any good at all in elections in Australia, but by 1965 it had managed to gain control over some of the biggest trade unions. With this control, it sought to undermine the nation's economy by calling strikes.

Thus, the nation was constantly disrupted by strike after strike. Almost always, they were only for a day or two. Occasionally, a major strike might take as much as a month before it broke. It was not so much the duration that troubled the population, it was the number of petty and pointless stoppages across all industries that happened week after week. Once again, I will keep you informed as we go about any major moves in this field, but remember that all citizens were annoyed almost daily by some group of workers who thought that they could create a better world by not working in this one.

MY RULES IN WRITING

Now we are just about ready to go. First, though, I give you a few Rules I follow as I write. They will help you understand where I an coming from.

NOTE. Throughout this book, I rely a lot on reproducing Letters from the newspapers. Whenever I do this, I put the text in a different font, and indent it a little, and make the font somewhat smaller. **I do not edit the text at all**. That is, I do not correct spelling or grammar, and if the text gets at all garbled, I do not correct it. It's just as it was seen in the Papers.

SECOND NOTE. The material for this book, when it comes from newspapers, is reported as it was seen at the time. If the benefit of hindsight over the years changes things, then I **might** record that in my **Comments**. The info reported thus reflects matters **as they were seen in 1966**.

THIRD NOTE. Let me also apologise in advance to anyone I might offend. In a work such as this, it is certain some people will think I got some things wrong. I am sure that I did, but please remember, all of this is **only my opinion**. And really, **my opinion does not matter one little bit in the scheme of things. I hope you will say "silly old bugger", and shrug your shoulders, and read on.**

So now we are ready to plunge into 1966. Let's go, and I trust you will have a pleasant trip.

JANUARY NEWS ITEMS

Doug Walters was a dashing Australian batsman, playing his second Test match against England in Melbourne. **In his first Test, he made a century. In this, his second Test, he did it again.** He was the first batsman since Bill Ponsford (in 1924) to score centuries in each of his first two Tests.

On December 19th, two **prisoners (Ronald Ryan and Peter Walker) escaped from Pentridge gaol** in Melbourne. They **killed a warder during the escape**, and four days later **robbed a bank** in the Melbourne suburb of Ormond. It is alleged that they also **killed an acquaintance**, a tow-truck driver, at Albert Park on Christmas Eve. The largest man-hunt in Victoria's history was launched by Victorian police....

Sydney, January 6. **Police arrested the two escapees in Sydney's Concord** in a planned operation after a tip-off. The pair were heavily armed, one of them fought until he "was knocked to the ground and was buried by the weight of ten burly detectives". The two men will be transported to Melbourne via a chartered plane.

A china figurine, on loan from **Royal Doulton potteries at Stoke-on-Trent in England**, depicts a **Spanish matador and a bull,** and is a large 28 inches long and 16 inches wide. It is valued at one thousand Pounds, and was **on display at David Jones' city store** in a glass case in the china shop....

This bull has now disappeared. Police are investigating, and the *SMH* at least was tickled by **the thought that there was now no bull in the china shop.**

The forces are massing in Vietnam. The US Senate estimates that the South Vietnam government has 600,000 troops involved. The US has 180,000 men. The baddies, the Viet Cong, have 230,000. There is no official estimate for China's involvement at the moment....

Australia at the moment has 12,000. Sadly, three of these were killed on January 9th. Two more were killed next day. Even sadder, there will be more deaths to come.

C-Day is almost here. Australia will switch to decimal currency on February 14th. The bank notes that will then be used are now on display. They were said to be "brighter with warmer colours", they were a "strong gutsy colour", and they were "an exciting piece of op art"....

January 15th. **Four million homes will receive a booklet** in the mail today describing how decimal currency will work. Seven "Dollar-Jills" will be employed to provide phone information about the currency.

January 29th. **Sir Robert Menzies resigned as Prime Minister** of Australia **after 16 years in office**. In a 55-minute TV presentation, he said he hoped to see more Test cricket, and that he was pleased to **"leave under his own steam". Harold Holt will succeed** him as Prime Minister.

Limes are a great fruit. You can use the Indian lime or the West Indian lime as a drink, or a garnish, or as a sauce, or as a flavour in cooking. Yet across the nation, it is hard to buy them. A recent search of the fruito shops in Hobart **showed no limes for sale**. A new industry is starting up.

A BEGINNER'S GUIDE TO VIETNAM

The fighting in Vietnam was an ideological battle between Capitalism and Communism. The Capitalists were mainly America and its allies such as Australia, backed up by the people of South Vietnam. The Communists were an undisclosed mixture of Reds, some of them Chinese, backed up by the people and government of North Vietnam. Both sides to the war said that they had the best system of everything, that they could run the world better than the other side, and that they could win more wars.

Of course, it was all mixed up with lots and lots of propaganda. In Australia, we were told that the Reds wanted to capture all the dominoes from Vietnam right down to Tasmania. We were told that they were inhuman monsters, that they would stop at nothing, that danger to us was always pressing, and that the might of the full Chinese Army was poised ready to enter the fray if we didn't manage to scare them off. The Reds were told similar things about the US and its allies, and were just as convinced as we were that **they** were the goodies.

The battle between the two sides was waging backward and forward. The military forces of North Vietnam were partly government sponsored, and partly by **a Communist group, called the Viet Cong**. It is this latter group that was at the forefront of the attacks on the South.

At the moment, the US had stopped its bombing of Viet Cong forces who had invaded the South. It had refrained for a period of 40 days. The stated reason for doing this was to show good faith so that their peace proposals might get a good hearing up North. Yet this matter was complicated because the same **US was refusing to talk to the Viet Cong**, saying that it was not the elected government of the North.

Meanwhile, it was increasing the number of troops that it had in Vietnam. Of course, no one knew how long the bombing reprieve would last.

The Reds too had made peace proposals, and there were conferences all over the place discussing all sides of the issues. Still, the fighting was going on, not full pelt, but this was little consolation for the men killed.

This simplistic description is enough to get us started. For more background, I enclose below a long Letter that sheds some light on why America wanted to be in Vietnam at all.

Letters, Edward Earl, Brisbane University. There are many reasons given for US involvement in Vietnam. All of these give a single simple reason, whereas the true reason is complex and ever-changing. Let me explain.

Some people would support the American action there because they believe that the Reds are a threat to South East Asia, and the Pacific. They remember Hitler, and think that if he had been stopped early, then there would have been no WWII. Others think that the only way to defeat Communism world-wide is to beat it militarily.

Others see it as an opportunity to spread Christianity. A powerful group wants to sell massive quantities of arms and munitions. Many in the armed forces hope to get rapid promotion in wartime. Some few resent all Asian influence in the USA.

Manufacturers of **all** goods see marketing opportunities if Asia is Americanised. Politicians, wrapping themselves in the flag, are counting the votes that will come with every bit of good news.

In fact, I could go on and on. So for people to say that there is **a single reason** for involvement is very **naïve and dangerously deceptive**.

I add that all of this will change with time. At the moment, the war is getting support (far from unanimous, though) from most Americans. This will change with time. As more Americans are killed, when the propaganda machine has to tell of mounting American losses, and as the scale of the bombings of Vietnam citizens become known, some of these groups above will drift to opposing the war.

Anyway, beware of those who say the Yanks are in for just one single reason. **Your speaker** may have just one reason, but the **nation** has many reasons.

We will re-visit Vietnam many times throughout this book.

ATTITUDE TO ASIANS

A Sydney woman saw a Red Cross van collecting blood from donors. She noticed a number of Asians waiting in the queue. She then wrote to the Press and said that the practice of taking blood from Asian donors was wrong, because it would make it impossible **to retain our racial purity**.

The volume of Letters in response was so great that the Editor of the *SMH* closed correspondence within two days. A few of them agreed with her, and then sprang to the then-familiar criticism of the Japanese, and their war atrocities. Others said that she was jumping at shadows, that blood does not work that way. They often added that we should hope that the getting of **new blood would improve us.**

In the final count, the Letters were almost universally condemnatory of the initial correspondent, and deeply apologetic towards any Asians who might have felt insulted by the Letter.

The event was interesting because it showed that the attitude to Asians, particularly to Japanese, had changed a great deal in the last decade. In 1954, most of the writers to Papers were still vocal in their hatred of the Japs, and wanted this nation to have nothing to do with them. It seems that, by now, much is forgotten and, perhaps less, forgiven.

Though, I must add that I have to hand a 2010 Letter, to myself, written by a woman who suffered the loss of her father and husband to the Japanese in 1944. She said she would rather die than accept blood from Japs.

THE POINT OF DECIMAL CURRENCY

The change over to decimal currency is about a month off. The actual day is February 14th, and it is called **C**-Day because that is the day when the **C**urrency changes. That means that, for example, 240 pennies in a Pound will convert to 200 cents in two dollars. Or, 120 pence in ten Shillings will convert to a dollar.

You would be wise to skip the detail. Half a dozen Letters a day were being written to the *SMH* complaining about how hard the conversion will be, and what dreadful complications will follow. I give you a tricky but typical example below.

Letters, Alan Boag. A spokesman for the petroleum industry was quoted during the weekend as saying that "any slight increase in petrol prices which could result from conversion to decimals could be almost totally overcome by motorists buying their requirements in "round figure' amounts," it was common for motorists to buy 1/ or 1 Pound worth of petrol now, and that these amounts would have their exact equivalent in dollars.

Let us examine the situation closely: Because the ruling price of premium grade petrol, 3/10, has no exact equivalent in decimal currency, the "slight increase" referred to by the anonymous spokesman would presumably be to 39 cents.

The motorist buying 10/ worth of petrol now gets 2.6 gallons. But if the petrol companies get their increase upon conversion to 39 cents, the motorist buying $1 worth will get only 2.3 gallons! The petrol companies will get an advantage of one-third of a gallon for every 10/ (or $) spent.

On the other hand, if the petrol companies accepted the monetary loss in a conversion of 3/10 to 38 cents the advantage to the motorist would amount to no more than .03 gallons for every $1 spent on petrol.

I trust the Prices Commissioner, Mr Newbigging, will take note of the situation brought to light by this analysis and not be misled by the petrol companies' specious reasoning.

Comment. If you have worked out what is going on in this case, I can give you another 100 to keep you occupied. The obvious point to everyone was that prices would rise in some cases, but less than one per cent. The Bush Lawyers found this hard to take, but most of the populace was happy to accept it with a slightly increased level of complaining.

The bank notes themselves provoked comments. Queen Elizabeth was on all of them. Others had images of John Macarthur, and Henry Lawson, and James Farrer. There were lots of other suggestions at this late stage.

Letters, L D Sames. It is a bad, sad day when Lachlan Macquarie, "The Father of Australia", was left off the new decimal currency banknotes. He was the first advocate for decimal currency, and his grand term of office as Governor of all Australia is one of the gems in our crown of history.

It is doubly ironical that his arch-enemy, John Macarthur, is pictured on this our first issue of the new currency. Surely the Bank of New South Wales, whose founding he called "his favourite measure", will have something to say about his absence.

Some people had other ideas. The most popular one was Don Bradman, followed by Les Darcy, and Phar Lap.

RENOUNCING CITIZENSHIP

Australia had welcomed about **two million migrants** to its shores since the war. More than half of these had come from Britain and a few thousand more had come from the British Commonwealth. None of these were required at any stage to renounce their former citizenship, and continued here with a dual passport.

For other migrants, most of whom were from Europe, various restrictions at various times applied. One such was that after a period of time, if they wanted to become naturalised Australian citizens, **they had to renounce their allegiance to their country of origin**. It is easy to understand that many people found this difficult to do.

One stumbling block was that, as migrants, they (or their family) **could not** be conscripted to join the Australian military forces. **As soon as they were naturalised**, they were put into the lottery pool from which our young National Servicemen were drawn. Right now this was a frightening thought for migrants with teenage boys because these youngsters, if so conscripted, could be sent off to fight in Vietnam.

The Letters below show a few sides of this difficult situation.

Letters, Dr C Wouters. Immigration authorities are quite right in thinking that **the renunciation of former allegiance is a powerful barrier** against many aliens applying for citizenship. Those who refuse to see that are blind with their eyes open.

It is my opinion that those conservative forces within the Liberal Party who stubbornly insist that aliens must continue to renounce their former country, are doing a lot of harm both to their party and the country they so vociferously pledge to serve.

Only a small percentage of migrants, out of resentment or indifference or for some unfathomable reason, may not care, but the vast majority feel a lump rise in their throats when they have to pronounce the humiliating and fatuous words of renunciation.

Letters, A V Fatseas. I am afraid it is a fallacious assumption that the 250,000 migrants still unnaturalised prefer to remain so for reasons of national conscience.

The renunciation of allegiance to their native countries, so far insisted upon when taking the oath of loyalty to the British Crown, may not be an easy pill to swallow, but is by no means the reason dissuading them from becoming Australian citizens.

The root of hesitancy is in that naturalisation carries with it obligations which loom fearsome in times of unsettled international situations such as the present – the very ones that drove hundreds of thousands from their own lands. A Greek, who left Greece to escape from the horrors of successive wars and endemic poverty, **could hardly be expected to view with enthusiasm the prospect of military conscription** in a land where he came to find peace and make money.

It seems to me there is no alternative to **enforcing** naturalisation; nor do I consider harsh any law which, after giving migrants five years of grace, **takes away the right to acquire any more property** from those who are not prepared to share in the defence of the country's institutions and the property they themselves own.

Letters, G Schmidt. Dr C Wouters' highly emotional outburst on the subject of renouncing former allegiances demands a public answer.

Having exercised my right as a free man to change my Dutch nationality into the Australian nationality, I had no option but to renounce my former allegiance.

It is legally, morally and logically impossible to accept a new nationality while still retaining a legal bond with a nationality ipso facto rejected! Or, in plain English, the **simple fact of applying for naturalisation means one renounces one's old allegiance.**

Dr Wouters and his ilk suffer from the delusion that they are forthwith forbidden to revere and respect or to have any sentimental feelings for their heritage. I cannot recollect this as being a condition for naturalisation.

It is they who are blind with their eyes open if they cannot see the difference between a legal act and an emotion.

Comment. For the moment I want to ignore the conscription side to this debate. Just suppose, though, that you went to live in France. You prospered there, you might or might not want to spend your later years there, or maybe back in Australia.

You would probably find that there were some benefits to assuming French nationality. **But would you renounce your Australian citizenship?** It's no easy decision, even apart from conscription issues.

INDEPENDENCE FOR NEW GUINEA

There is a great big island off the top of Australia. It was more or less agreed that the western half was part of Indonesia, and it was fully agreed that the eastern half was controlled by Australia under a protectorate from the United Nations.

In 1966, half the nations in the world were blinking at the light and saying that it was time they put some serious thought into gaining their independence, or controlling their own resources, and adopting different forms of government.

New Guinea was not one of those nations. The riots and revolutions that were sweeping the black nations in Africa were nowhere to be seen. Still, in a more peaceful way, the progress to a different constitutional life there was subject to increasing debate. A new House of Assembly had been created with elected Members, and its role was to work towards independence for the protectorate. At a recent meeting, it was **suggested that the Territory should become an Australian State**.

The Editor of the *SMH* was emphatic in his **arguments against this**. He argued that, at a time when the world was revolting against imperialism, Australia would be seen as now stealing another black nation for itself. He went on to say that there was no evidence that the population wanted this move. He saw it as a move by an elite conservative minority to feather their own nests. He thought that the result might lead to rebellion and turmoil, as had happened in a similar situation between France and Algeria.

Then, he continued, if it happened, Australia would have a boundary with Indonesia, and that might not be desirable. Finally, he considered that the future of New Guinea lay with Melanesia, and not with the European society of Australia.

These were pretty good arguments against the proposal. But a few people still thought it worthy.

Letters, U Ewart. Why should not the Territory of Papua-New Guinea ultimately become a seventh State of the Commonwealth? Your editorial says it would be called "neo-colonialism" by Asian and other nations.

But why? On what grounds, provided Statehood was mutually desired by the Territory and Australia? Have we become so spineless as to base our policies on the catchcries of totalitarian dictatorships (for that is the source of this particular cry)?

You suggest that the lesson of twentieth-century history is that new statehood could only lead to bitterness and recrimination and maybe to rebellion and turmoil. What a pessimistic view! How scornful it is of the sterling work of the Department of Territories, and of the Administration and indigenous leaders, that clearly shows dedication to the task of nation-building. Why should not Australia be a history-maker in this field, as she has already shown she can be in others?

Why should we not be willing to share, and the peoples of the Territory accept, the benefits of a mutual defence umbrella, common postal, Customs, civil aviation and other matters of the Federal structure? **It is certain that unless we have a plan for Papua-New Guinea, some other nation will**. Our statesmen and Territory leaders have a great opportunity now to formulate a bold, imaginative plan for the future, and this might well be based on the idea of ultimate statehood.

Letters, Jack Lusby.   At the present time, most Papua-New Guinea indigenes accept and trust the Administration officers and the many other Australians living and working among them. As the horizons of the more sophisticated natives widen, these people feel incomparably closer to Australia in every way than to any other nation.

Even a few years ago in 1953-54, when I saw most parts of the New Guinea highlands where white faces were still something of a novelty, hill-men I came to know well were quick to show a lively interest in the home country of the Australians. In 1954 two highland chiefs flew to Cairns in Queensland to meet Queen

Elizabeth. On the day of their return to Mount Hagen, thousands of mountain tribesmen crowded the airstrip to conduct an on-the-spot interrogation, orderly and prolonged, about the Australian way of life and our link with the Queen.

The objection that, as an Australian State, Papua-New Guinea would border directly on a potentially hostile country seems of minor consequence in the modern concept of warfare. It could, in fact, be strategically desirable to have a clear view of our neighbour's backyard.

Comment. As you know, PNG is now an independent nation with its own seat at the UN. Australia retains close ties with it, and renders much assistance and Foreign Aid.

NEWS AND VIEWS

Oz TV. Really? Letters. We have 90 hours a week of TV between the hours of 7pm and close. Of these, 72 hours are drama. Of these, 10 are British, 72 are US and **only one is Australian**.

Our sole production is _Homicide_ which is proving most popular, even though it is made on a limited budget. That is why we have such low employment of actors, writers and directors compared to other countries.

No country in the world rejects its own actors, writers and composers more than Australia. No city in the world employs Australia's rejected talent more than London.

New Guinea Statehood. Letters. NG has a population of over two million. If it became a state of Australia on an equal basis, then you would expect about a million of these fine people to **cross over into Australia proper overnight**. Are we prepared for that?

January 22nd. **58 clergymen**, many of them prominent, have signed a statement, to be released in New York today, calling on the US **to end the horror of the Vietnam war**.

Three young children, surnamed Beaumont, were taken from their home in Adelaide on January 27th. Police suspect that they **have been murdered. Comment.** Their bodies have never been recovered despite many extensive searches.

Slow start at the races. The start of the first race at Melbourne's Flemington racetrack was delayed today. This was because a perfectly dressed man, in a suit and tie and hat, ducked under the rail near the starter's gate, with a shot gun. **He fired one shot into the air and threatened all and sundry to fire again.**

He was the 52-year-old son of one of Melbourne's most respected trainers. He wanted a guarantee that "the jockeys would keep both hands on their horses during the races". That means **he wanted to stop the jockeys from using whips.** He surrendered to police after 10 minutes.

FEBRUARY NEWS ITEMS

Oh Dear. After a lull of 38 days, the Americans re-started the bombing of military and communications targets in North Vietnam. As President Johnson said, they were doing this in the "determined and unremitting pursuit of peace". The hope is that the threat of heavy bombings will "open the way to the conference table". The US military will no longer release the information on the quantity of bombs dropped each day.

Britain is having a hard time economically, and wants to **cut the cost of its military commitments in all countries** "east of Suez." That means Australia and New Zealand as well as Singapore and Malaya and other smaller nations and colonies....

Early in February, there will be defence talks in Canberra. There the Poms will put concrete proposals to the Oz Government. They are really saying that **we are on our own in matters of defence. They put it nicely**. They say that they will "**offer us complete independence in defence matters**". Who could refuse an offer of independence? In fact, Australia will not, because we have no choice in this delicate matter.

Here's a bit of news **for the old-timers**. American film personality, **comedian Buster Keaton, died** in Hollywood, aged 70 on February 2nd.

February 4th. **The Russians landed the first space craft, Luna-2, on the moon**, and it is transmitting pictures. The event was widely acclaimed, and even **the US President was generous in his congratulations to Russia.**

The sponsors **of a Bikini Girl contest**, at the land-locked city of Wagga Wagga in NSW, were refused permission to hold the contest at the local "beach" on a nearby river. **The local Council said no to their application. The local Catholic Bishop ordered Catholic girls not to enter the contest.** But some did, and **800 people turned up to watch** the girls parade at the Town Hall. The contest was won by a slim, black-headed woman, a former model. **She is a Catholic.**

Just a reminder that life goes on. The *Age* headline for February 8th said "Transport, gas and power strikes to halt Victoria for two days".

H G Palmer had been prominent for a decade during which **Hire Purchase** and the **introduction of TV** have cajoled much money from consumers. On February 10th, the **chain closed another 24 stores round Australia**, and the remainder are under administration. There are many unhappy creditors, and **also thousands of debenture holders** who are much poorer than they were before.

Businesses began collecting **one and two cent pieces from banks** in large quantities. **They will need these for change** when C-day arrives next Monday.

A month ago, a US bomber took off from Spain and then **crashed into the sea** near the coast. It was carrying an atomic bomb, and **was found in 1,000 feet of water. A US mini-sub is now moving to recover the bomb.** Shore areas nearby are being "suitably controlled in case of damage".

The Labor Party continues to be deeply divided. **That is not news.** On February 12th, the Central Executive of the

Party again said that it was **against** any form of **State aid** to religious schools. **That too is not news**....

What is news is that the Deputy Leader of the Party, **Gough Whitlam, made an emphatic statement that he is in favour of aid**. This is in direct defiance of the Executive, and it is likely that he will be called up for discipline. He was in **breach of ALP rules**, and shows an attitude not often seen in the Party. Keep your eye on this man. He could become a new broom, and **he might be going places.**

February 18th. **Change-over to decimal currency went smoothly**, except for petty niggles on the price of boxes of matches and the like. One spectacular result was that **the banks were flooded with useless pennies**, which can be converted to cents at banks....

For example, today the Bank of NSW in five hours of trading **cashed in 48 tons of pennies**. In Sydney, six armoured cars were kept busy all day, and into the night, ferrying pennies from the branches to Head Office.

The world's biggest cattle station, the 7-million acre Alexander Downs in the Northern Territory, is to be sub-divided and some sold. It is 150 miles long.

As the month passed, **Whitlam** gained more support for a bid for Labor leadership. He **might be ready to challenge Arthur Calwell**. The Liberals, on the other hand, are getting more cautious. They **were** thinking of calling an early election. But they think that if Whitlam wins the leadership, **Labor will be a more formidable an opponent**. Exciting times in politics. **We will wait and see.**

STRIKE ACTION IN VICTORIA

The nation was outraged by the **Public Servants** in Victoria calling a two-day strike calculated to get them a four-week annual holiday. This particularly hurt persons using public transport, as well as a myriad of government services such as Land Tax offices, and Births, Deaths and Marriages.

The Public Servants were seen by most people as having a **very comfortable job** already, with good working conditions, good salaries, good allowances, good holidays, and security of tenure. They were often seen as pampered, and often unhelpful and bureaucratic, and sometimes positively rude and indifferent at the counter. In short, if the Labor movement wanted to start a campaign for longer holidays, this was not the group to start with.

But they did. The reaction was widespread and very hostile as these three Letters from Victoria attest.

Letters, Harry H Benchwyn. What would be the attitude of **earlier** trade unionists to the happenings in Victoria this week? These men achieved the 8-hour day, and the principle of holidays with pay with great personal sacrifice and the risk of victimisation. But they would probably **have chosen to fight the great monopolies** or prosperous industries like steel, chemicals, or the motor industry, before picking on public utilities.

It is hard to understand the Trades Hall Council, whom one would expect would stand for equality, rather than support the perpetuation of a **privileged class of public employees**.

One is tempted to believe that some of the leaders have the childish notion of bringing down the present Government with acts like these, of the "rolling strikes" of recent times in certain branches of the transport industries, obviously overlooking that conditions in Australia, 1966, are somewhat different from those of the working classes of Czarist Russia in 1917.

It is very hard to make sense of the whole affair.

Letters, M Campbell. How long will the people of Victoria put up with such unwarranted and childish strikes by State Government workers for four weeks' holidays with pay? It is time the people took action.

Four weeks' holidays, indeed. Soon they will be asking each other, not "when are you taking your holidays this year?", but "when are you working this year?" They have more public holidays, sick time allowances, &c., than the average working man.

What will be the result if four weeks' holiday with pay be granted (heaven forbid)? It will mean rises in train, tram, gas, electricity, coal &c., and eventually a general lowering of living standards. Besides having to pay these increased costs, food will probably rise also.

It is time, too, Mr Jordan and his colleagues at the THC did something worthwhile to justify their salaries paid by unionists, instead of calling idle strikes such as the present one. No one to whom I have spoken on this subject has been in favour of it. Most are definitely against it.

Letters, Archie Michaelis. Among those of us who are not smiling are those hundreds of thousands of bread-winners, many paying off homes with other commitments, young mothers with clothes to wash and hot baths to provide, not to mention all those whose businesses necessitates the use of trams or buses. Then there are also the school children and others who cannot afford to drive cars or to drive in them.

What is the object of the exercise? To give Government employees, already well-treated and with many super rights, a further advantage over their fellows by way of longer leave?

It is surprising that the unionists don't tell their committees to stop being fooled.

Comment. It is a sad fact that such strikes, and similar responses, were repeated day after day in every State in Australia. To the person in the home, it was all so silly. **What could be achieved by such actions?** There was no hope of the workers all combining into a revolutionary force and taking control of government. Why did the ordinary workers go along with the Reds who were inspiring these strikes? Because if they stepped out of line, the Reds were well organised and could make their lives hell. It just wasn't worthwhile to put your livelihood in danger. For example, what man, and his family, **wanted to be branded a scab**?

So, the strike situation will continue on throughout the year. **You need to keep it in mind all the time**, even though I will not take up valuable space talking about the various events as they occur.

THE VIETNAM STORY: EARLY DAYS

In my Introduction, I gave you enough background to get you off the ground. This month, I would like to add to that by pointing out some of the passions that were being raised within Australian society by the issue, even at this early stage. You will see as we go along that there are many different facets to this story. My aim, without becoming obsessive about the War, is to give you an adequate grasp of many of them.

The first item concerns the US Ambassador to Australia, Mr Edward Clark. He had just returned to Australia after a trip to Washington, where he was fully briefed on plans for Vietnam.

When questioned by the Press, he gave nothing away, but he did comment on what he said the American public was thinking. Below is an Australian's response to his answer.

Letters, N Baker.   Mr Clark stated on his return from America that Americans were most anxious to know whether the Australian public supported them in Vietnam. He said that the question of Australian support was being asked from "top to bottom – from the President to the most callow schoolboy." According to your report, Mr Clark stated that he was able to look every questioner in the eye and say Australia supported America without shirking.

If Mr Clark really thinks this, he must be without doubt the most uninformed or misinformed US Ambassador ever to be sent to Australia.

Of my fairly wide acquaintance of Australians of many groups, professional people of high reputation (and very conservative politics) to people in more humble occupations on the basic wage, it is my considered opinion that a majority of these people have very serious doubts about American policies and aims in Vietnam.

It is a serious reflection on the present state of democracy in Australia that, of this majority, many feel that they have no adequate way of expressing this dissatisfaction (they are not the type to take part in protest marches) and many others feel frightened – yes, frightened – to express their views publicly for fear of being branded "Commo."

Next we have a Letter from a well known **journalist** called Alan Ashbolt. He was an avid commentator on current affairs, who was violently against the war. He had earlier been prominent in founding the *ABC's Four Corners* programme, and thereafter he had continued a love-hate relationship with the *ABC*, which saw him time and again fighting with the management there.

He wrote a letter to the *SMH* apologising for his behaviour at a rowdy meeting held in St John's Hall in the Sydney suburb of Gordon. This was a wealthy and very respectable suburb that normally was loath to get into the news. The meeting was called to protest against the Vietnam war.

He described how he went along to the meeting to hear another journalist, Francis James, tell of his recent experiences in Hanoi and Saigon, and was expecting to hear much more of the truth than the newspapers were presenting.

However, a Mr Arthur Smith jumped onto the platform and by his shouting and attempts to take over the microphone, it was clear that he wanted to disrupt the meeting. Mr Smith was the leader of the Australian Nazi Party.

This upset Mr Ashbolt. Firstly, because about 30 per cent of the audience, by their shouts and jeers, appeared to support Mr Smith. These were all about 20 years of age, and were doubtless imported to Gordon with the intention of disrupting the meeting. Secondly, beause he knew that the speaker was a war veteran with a distinguished record. He was so incensed by the lack of respect given to Mr James that he jumped onto the stage, and joined in the jostling that was by now happening. He wanted to defend Mr Jame's integrity, and to prevent the break up of the meeting.

Angry scenes followed, in which Mr Ashbolt was involved. Mr Smith was removed by police. The meeting fell apart, and Mr Ashbolt was **now** apologising for his impetuous intervention, but was saying that he always gets angry when freedom of speech was threatened.

Mr Ashbolt's letter was a turning point in the reportage of the War. Prior to that, fracas at demonstrations were reported as just minor punch-ups. After Ashbolt, the *SMH* and others treated them as part of an ongoing argument over the War, and saw to it that public protest was kept in the forefront of the mind of the public. **The demo was taking on its own news value.**

Comment. Apart from that, you can see that tempers were running high, and that there were all sorts of players getting involved.

As an aside. The Francis James mentioned was another journalist, who was intent upon talking about his recent trip to Vietnam. He was a notable figure, who commonly appeared in public wearing a large-brimmed black hat and a black cloak. From 1950, he was involved with writing for the *SMH*, *The Anglican*, and *Oz* magazine. In 1969, he was **arrested in China, allegedly for spying**, and remained in prison for four years, until he was released after his school friend, Gough Whitlam, lobbied for his release. **The war had some heavy-weight activists, for and against.**

Back to the main story. A couple of writers who witnessed the Gordon row had their say.

Letters, J F Moseley. Like Allan Ashbolt, I went to St John's Hall, Gordon, last Thursday evening, to learn about Vietnam. Francis James is an ornament to the profession of journalism; he is a good observer, and only a month ago visited the scene that so deeply concerns us. His address was excellent, and could not have been more objective and unbiased.

I learnt a lot about Vietnam, but I also learnt a lot about Gordon, and Australia. The hall was full, and I never doubted that everybody there was interested in hearing a first-hand account by a reliable eye-witness of the place on which our attention is focused. **I was mistaken**; **it turned out** that a large section of the audience had come to try to prevent this objective, unbiased view being presented.

Another writer brought Bob Menzies into the argument. "I was at this meeting and I feel that Mr Ashbolt was rightly angered at the attempt of Mr Smith to take over the meeting. I was also angered not so much by the actions of Mr Smith, but by the remarks made by Mr James about our former Prime Minister, Sir Robert Menzies. I registered my protest by walking out of the meeting as did about 80 per cent of the audience present."

Comment. I asked you **a moment ago** to keep in mind that **strikes** were just part of the background all over the nation. **Now** I ask you to remember, as you read this book, that **meetings, and demos such as this, were growing in number and would continue to do so for years**. Every capital city, and every regional city, had one or a dozen such meetings every week-end. If you wanted to shout abuse, or hoot and boo, this was the place to go. If you were bearing a placard, and wanted it to be pushed up your left nostril, then look no further. If you were a bit strange, and wanted clear and logical comments on some Vietnam issue, you were in the wrong place.

A MESSAGE FROM BY-GONE DAYS?

The Letter below reminds me of a way of courting that satisfied many people in 1966.

Letters, Mrs Estella P McKenzie, Deer Park. I was very interested, though a little alarmed, over the article by Alan Nicolls in "The Age" on juvenile promiscuity, and I commend the letter by Philip Opas in reply.

I was, for a number of years, the secretary of an Anglican church youth club consisting of members of both sexes. The club activities were many and varied – social, physical, intellectual and mental aspects being the aim.

As members, we were also expected to attend church services, and most did, even if it were to talk to the pretty girl or attractive youth sitting next to one.

I don't remember any one of the hundreds we met at group meetings, dances and so on, being thought a "square" or "snob" or "spoil sport." There was much interest in the opposite sex and as I remember, there was only **one** member who was suddenly and quietly married.

If young people take an active interest in, and belong to, one or more of the many sports clubs, drama groups, musical societies, adult education groups, &c., then there is little time or occasion for promiscuity.

Besides, they will be taking part in healthy activities. They will be meeting other young people with similar healthy interests and healthy minds in healthy bodies usually result.

What better way to meet one's life partner instead of so many young people either having illegitimate children or marrying at 17 or 18 years and then regretting it in a few years' time?

Comment. Are there **still** many young folk who meet people this way? Or have those civilised days gone forever? Or am I being just a nostalgic old fool who is clinging to fond memories, and who thinks that what was good enough for me should be the right thing forever?

LETTERS IN BRIEF

A plea for square coins. **Letters.** For about a year, the old currency and the new decimal currency will **both** be in circulation. This will be a nightmare for everyone, and especially for people like bus conductors who have to give change quickly.

I suggest that the news coins be made so that they are square, or square with rounded edges. I should not have to argue the benefits of this. If you can tell me why we need **round** coins, then you can forget the square. But if you can't, then they should all be square or squared.

Get rid of dogs. **Letters.** At the Sydney inner beach of Balmoral, dogs are persistently dumped, and stay alive only because of the food that persons like myself give them.

These dogs are beautiful creatures, and many would find good homes if people were aware of them. So I suggest that **loud-speakers be erected at the beach**, and every hour the description of a few dogs be announced. I am sure that the swimmers and sun-bakers would not be disturbed by these announcements, and would at the same time welcome them in the knowledge that they are serving an excellent purpose.

Dogs beware of the hand that feeds. **Letters.** Your writer who feeds dogs at Balmoral will doubtlessly think he is doing a good thing. But he should listen to this advice.

A year ago we adopted a dog from a pound, and we fed it, and de-flead it, and gave it a good kennel, and paid its several vet bills, and loved it. We live less that a mile from Balmoral beach, and so the grapevine told our dog that free meals were on offer at the beach.

So our dog started to go missing in the middle of the day, and now it goes away for periods of three days or more. It comes back looking fatter and fatter.

Apart **from breaking up the family**, your kind donor of food should be aware that feeding a dog with sandwiches and biscuits, and the like, is destroying his health. Our alternative is to chain him all the time. Or donors could stop donating.

Migration from NG to Australia. **Letters.** A writer last month said that, if New Guinea became a state of Australia, there would be a one-way flood of citizens into Australia.

I have lived in New Guinea for decades. No one, black or white, would give up living here for the uncertain benefits of living in the mainland. People who visit Australia regularly or only rarely, come back with horrible or laughable stories of the follies of Australia proper.

The number who would want to change over is virtually zero.

A ridiculous suggestion. **Letters.** A visiting American banker came up with this load of nonsense. He said "the cheque system is on the way out. The charge card is the way of tomorrow".

Two-up can still be played. **Letters.** Many writers asked if two-up would die out if there were no longer any pennies round. A number of writers replied, in all seriousness, that it would be possible to still keep a store of pennies for that purpose. One writer said the two-cent coin would be no use for playing, because the possum on the coin made one side heavier than the other, and would introduce bias.

Other writers said that the 50 cent coin would be big enough to use. Experienced gamblers pointed out that two 50 cent coins would be too big for the kip. In any case, if they rolled, they would get stolen.

One writer added, for free, these words of wisdom. A member of the British gentry, called Lord Hertford, was asked what he would do if he saw a man cheating at cards. He replied "bet on him, that's for sure"

Horse troughs. **Letters,** Tom Mix. Twenty years ago, every town in this nation had one or more concrete troughs where a horse could stop and get a good drink of water. Some bigger towns had dozens, and the streets of the cities had them every half mile.

So I ask, what happened to them? I am not asking **why** did they disappear. The answer to that lies in the fact that horses have all been sent to the glue factory.

What I want to know is, **where did they all go to?** They are not the type of thing that a single person can move. It must have been several men with a truck. Did Councils have a pick-up and drive them to the local dump? Has an enterprising gang stolen them and is hoarding them now, waiting for horses to make a comeback?

Let me point out that I have visited three museums in the last few years, and there are no horse troughs there. So, I ask, where did they all go?

Tragedies. 24 children and four adults were killed when an avalanche of **colliery** waste engulfed a school and houses in a Welsh mining village.

On the same day, four coal miners were killed in a pit near a small NSW town of Abermain.

Darwin. Max Daniels, a carpenter, has become the **first Aboriginal to be awarded a prestigious Churchill scholarship.**

MARCH NEWS ITEMS

March 1st. Architect **Joern Utzon quit as designer of the Sydney Opera House.** It is believed that this move was prompted by Ministerial efforts to control costs….

Initially, in 1957, the cost was estimated **at 6 million dollars**, and construction time was to be **five years.** In 1966, the cost has **risen to over 50 million**, and the completion time will not be in the next two years….

March 4th. 4,000 architects, students and supporters **marched in Sydney in protest against the resignation of Utzon.** They presented a signed-by-all **petition** to Premier Askin, **asking for his reinstatement.** After a week of negotiating, his resignation was confirmed.

The **four-day Australian Open Golf Tournament will end on a Sunday** this year. This is the first time ever. It follows a similar move for the British Open this year.

The Full Bench of **the Australian Arbitration Commission,** chaired by its President, **Sir Richard Kirby,** decided to grant **equal pay and working conditions to some full-blooded Aborigines** working on cattle stations in the Northern Territory. This will raise their rate of pay from about $10 per day to $20….

The Bench pointed out that a large proportion of the Aboriginal population was impeded by cultural **and tribal reasons** from appreciating the concept of work. **Still, the situation was changing,** and it was time for equal pay.

March 10th. The Government announced that Australia will **treble its forces in Vietnam to 4,500** by June this year. **Conscripted National Servicemen will be included….**

Opposition Leader, **Arthur Calwell, demanded a referendum** on **conscripting** into *the war zone.*

He said that the Government wanted to send "**voteless conscript boys against their wills to die in Vietnam**" and was, at the same time, "breaking its neck to increase its exports of wool and metals to Communist China."

The Federal Government **made a big dent in White Australia Policy by relaxation of the immigration laws for non-Europeans. Firstly**, the qualification for temporary residence were changed from "well-qualified and distinguished" to "well qualified and **useful**". This allowed the entry of scientists and academics, for example....

Secondly, for existing temporary residents, it reduced the qualifying period of residence applying for citizenship. The change was **from 15 years to 5 years**. This will allow 2,100 persons to apply immediately.

A **new oil discovery** off the coast in **the Gippsland area of Victoria** has produced good flows. The well is owned by BHP, in conjunction with Esso. Woodside Oil owns an adjacent lease. **Shares of the Australian companies boomed today.**

Crowds were demonstrating against involvement in Vietnam, with a focus on the sending of **conscript**s. In Sydney, 2,000 persons turned out. A few young men burned their registration cards which they were given to prove that they had registered for service. **The famous slogan "Make love, not war" was starting to be seen.**

On March 18th, a **660lb high-explosive German mine from WWII washed ashore** at Surfers Paradise in Queensland.

After a few days of consideration, it was decided **to tow it a distance of five miles along the beach** to a safer place, to detonate it....

News of this spread, and when a young Navy Lieutenant started to drive the tractor that would move the mine, **a crowd of 20,000 people were there to applaud him and cheer him on.** This dangerous mission, with a booby-trapped mine, was done without a hitch. So, too, was the later demolition.

March 25th. The Government announced that **youths who burned their draft cards would be liable to a fine of 100 Dollars**. It also said that if these same youths had been granted a deferment for some time, their deferment would be cancelled and the youths, if medically fit, would be called up immediately....

Remember that the general process for calling up youths was to have **their birthdays drawn from a barrel**. If your birthday was pulled out, then you would be called up. But if you burned your card, **you would automatically skip the ballot, and go straight into the forces**.

A man-made **flying machine**, looking suspiciously like a Hills Hoist, was tested over the weekend in Adelaide. A former cycling champion, Wally Smith, perched in the middle, **was peddling furiously, hoping to get elevation**....

The craft, called the "kookaburra", trundled up and down the field, but **failed to lift off**. The attempt was ended when he got a puncture. He will try again, and his aim is to win **a 13,000 Pound prize offered in England for a man-powered flight of a mile.**

UTZON: THE STORY

The Askin government had recently been elected to run NSW, and the new Minster in charge of the Opera House, David Hughes, was very conscious of the great blow-out in costs. Utzon had been spending money, quite legitimately, for materials to do the job, but had not been getting formal approval.

When Hughes came to office, Utzon presented him with a bill for 100,000 dollars for these materials, and Hughes refused to pay because they had not been approved. This situation was made worse because Utzon insisted on having a certain type of plywood for the concert theatre, because it reflected sound in a favourable way. Again Hughes refused, saying the same effect could be achieved by less costly materials.

Of course, this was just what the public was told. There were probably other matters as well. In any case, Utzon resigned. For about ten days, Premier Askin talked with the two men, trying to find a middle way. They ended up having another meeting. For a while it seemed that the two above problems could be fixed, but Hughes insisted that Utzon surrender his one-man control of the project, and in future **be directed by a committee** of architects and accountants. Utzon refused, not surprisingly, and so his resignation stood.

UTZON: THE PUBLIC REACTION

Let me say first up that there was huge interest in what was going on. The nation's newspapers were flooded with Letters, and radio and TV was full of all sorts of stories, some of them true. The *SMH* on two days devoted two entire Letters pages to the story, with liberal column space on a dozen other days.

The range of opinions was vast. Some would have supported Utzon if he had built an Ark. Others hated everything about him, including the manner of his selection in the first place. In between, more rational writers regretted the cost blow-out, and some blamed his wild dreaming for this. Others said that he was brilliant, and that given a unique edifice would grace Sydney for all time, cost should be no object. Then others said that surely it was the expert Utzon who should decide on technical matters such as plywoods, and that Hughes should stick to politics.

In any case, let me pick out just a few Letters to show their diversity.

Letters, A Carter. The plans for the **Taj Mahal** were prepared by a **council** of architects from India, Persia, Central Asia and beyond, but that did not prevent it from being a very fine and successful building.

So far as giving Mr Utzon carte blanche is concerned, that would be ridiculous. In inquiring into costs and procedures for which he must ultimately take responsibility, the Minister for Public Works, Mr Hughes, was only doing his duty.

Letters, Eva Buhrich. Once again political power-juggling, professional jealousy and narrow-minded bureaucracy are driving a man of genius from our midst. Thirty years ago it was Walter Burley Griffin and now it is Utzon.

We are trying to break the man, a creative architect of world reputation, and to spoil his work, one of the great buildings of our time.

But no doubt in 20 years, when a lot of water will have washed past the Opera House, and today's politicians will have been forgotten, we will make amends and, as with Griffin, honour Utzon on one of our postage stamps. For such is the size of our vision.

Letters, W Warden. From the turning of the first sod of soil on two acres of Sydney's fast disappearing parklands, till the present, the whole scheme has been a colossal and disgraceful waste of public money and resources. The method of raising the money, 100,000 Pound lotteries, is morally doubtful and has been directly responsible for one murder that we know of.

Surely now is the time to stop work on this monument to irresponsible Government spending, and channel the money so saved into essential services. A few that come easily to mind, more so lately as we've heard so much about the shortage of money for them, are the Eastern Suburbs railway, sewage disposal, water supply State-wide, country roads and teacher training.

It is obvious by now that to start this Benelong Point project was a mistake. It is time for the Government to be honest with itself and admit it, and stop work on it before any more hard cash is swallowed up.

Letters, (Mrs) J S Horn. It is to be profoundly hoped that the Government of NSW will prevail upon Mr Utzon to stay and finish the Opera House. His departure now would be a national tragedy. The thought of anyone else – however competent – stepping in to finish the brilliant and inspired conception which is Utzon's alone, is utterly appalling.

The Opera House has already cost millions – painlessly extracted from a willing public. Let it cost a bit more and be finished in the same inspired manner of high perfection in which it was conceived and begun.

Letters, F E Starley. There are, in Sydney, many fine architects who are sufficiently competent to do the best which can be done with this unfortunate project. They should, however, be selected for their integrity and not for their compliance to directives.

To date, less than 30 per cent of the ultimate cost has been incurred, so **it is still not too late to quit** the present plan and to erect a building more suited to the dynamic cultural needs of the people of New South Wales – and matched to their resources.

Letters, Jim Coleman, Bruce Bowden, Vivian Fraser. If the original concept is to be brought to reality, if the design team is to remain at their drawing boards, and if the people of New South Wales are to get the building they asked for nine years ago, Mr Utzon must be persuaded to stay on and finish the job. It is inconceivable that any other architect could achieve such an end.

We therefore see it as the duty of the citizens of this State to press for an immediate relaxation of the tension existing between Parliament House and Benelong Point, and to do all in their power to convince Jorn Utzon that we, the people, are worthy of his continuing services as the architect of one of the great buildings of all time.

Other writers suggested that the keys of the Treasury be handed over to Utzon, and just let him spend as he will. A group of 16 architects believed that no architect would be crass and disloyal enough to accept Utzon's position. One hearty soul thought that the Minister for Public Works should be cheered by all persons in NSW.

Comment. Mr Utzon did **not** withdraw his resignation, and he **did** leave his position. In case you need telling, the Opera House was completed and is quite splendid.

As one writer put it "On a visit to Sydney from Darwin, I can see that the Opera House when finished will be a great spot for a concert. I will agitate, when I get back to Darwin, to get one for ourselves".

VIETNAM: FUN IN THE PARKS

Let me explain how many Australians felt about Vietnam. Take the household with a nineteen-year-old male. This lad, probable as silly as a rattlesnake, and fun-loving and carefree to the point on inanity, is now approaching his twentieth birthday with dread. Soon after that day, his birthday is drawn out of a barrel, and he will be forced into the armed services.

After three months of basic training, he will probably be sent off to Vietnam, and there he might be maimed or killed.

This is what mothers and fathers, sisters, brothers, girl-friends, and the boys themselves, saw on the horizon. Most of them hardly knew where Vietnam was, even fewer were worried about the domino effect of the Reds maybe taking over Australia at some time in the future, and none of them were worried by that thought.

So, to these people, and their many friends, the situation had suddenly become a matter of life and death – literally. They could not accept this conscription, they had to do something. Being Australia, the way they could do this was to demonstrate with thousands of others in the same boat.

So, demonstrations and meetings of protest were popping up everywhere, right across the nation. Hundreds, sometimes thousands, of people marched the streets chanting slogans, and waving placards. Parks were filled with speakers, hymns were sung, and prayers en masse were said. **The demo had arrived**, and the demos were soon to get bigger.

Some, however, thought that the Yanks were right to intervene in Vietnam, and some others thought that Australia must do its bit to fight the Red advance. So these people joined the same demos, intent on disrupting them. Ratbag elements joined in, perhaps Reds, or perhaps seeking to reinstate the fallen Nazi Party, or perhaps wanting better treatment for chooks. The inevitable punch-ups followed, and the newspapers and media did their best to inflame the situation.

It would have been good clean fun, and a good example of how a democracy should work, if the subject at hand had not been the lives of our young men.

So, back to Vietnam. **Firstly,** Letters on conscription.

Letters, K Couchman. As a long-time supporter of the Liberal Party, I must applaud the stand taken by the Leader of the Opposition, Mr Calwell, in demanding a **referendum** on sending conscripts abroad.

Even in the early stages of the last world war, **men called up were kept for home defence**. This makes the present decision of the Holt Government even more overbearing. Also it is at least a debatable question as to whether or not Australian troops should be in Vietnam. Is it right to ask a conscripted Australian boy to fight and die for anything as elusive as Australian aims in Vietnam?

However, regardless of any opinions concerning this present jungle war, the fact remains that this decision is taken without any mandate from the people and many voters, like myself, must wonder how their voices can be heard in this democratic State.

To clarify the other point, I should say that if the Regular Army is a man's chosen vocation, then he should go to **any** theatre determined by his Government. To send **conscripts**, however, at this time is an undemocratic violation of personal rights.

Letters, (Miss) W Christison. The leader of the Opposition, Mr Calwell, is concerned over the sending of "voteless conscript youths" to fight in South Vietnam, as they "have never been asked whether or not they wished to fight and die in an unwinnable jungle war."

May I be permitted to ask how a referendum would solve the problem he sees, for, as he says, these youths are voteless, and since when has any parent been able to deduce accurately precisely what goes on in the mind of an 18 or 20-year-old?

Letters, (Mrs) Anne Barker. Now that the Government has decided it is necessary to send National Service trainees to Vietnam, it is certainly time that the unfair ballot system is altered. While realising how important it is for university students to complete their studies, when it comes to a matter of life and death, as it does now in Vietnam, surely **all** sections of the community should be equally involved rather than penalising the less educated. Surely in this day and age a plumber is as good as a university graduate.

Then there are the ugly scenes in the parks. You saw last month the example of a meeting at Gordon. I will follow that up with this description of another charming scene.

Letters, Michael Darby. In respect of the article "fists fly during Vietnam speech" there are a number of points which should be clarified, which I shall deal with in the order presented by the article.

The police who arrived at the meeting called on behalf of a young man who was assaulted and had his clothing torn when he rose to sing the National Anthem. The police were not called by the organisers of the meeting.

When it was learned before the meeting that no arrangements for the National Anthem had been made, a young pianist requested permission to play the Anthem as if it were a scheduled part of the program. Permission was refused. A number of people, myself included, when the meeting was due to commence, rose and began to sing "God Save The Queen." We were joined by about 200 members of the audience who were subjected, while singing, to a barrage of insults and abuse from all sides. It was at this point that the young man was attacked. The chairman then authorised that the National Anthem be sung again.

After the speaker had made certain references to the United States, the Australian and USA flags were raised. An attack was immediately launched by ruffians who punched, kicked and swore in an endeavour to seize the flags. No blows were struck by anyone expressing support for the United States.

I left the meeting of my own accord, disgusted by the standover tactics used to repress any expression of support for Australia and the United States. About 150 others also walked out in protest.

I do not believe that the violent elements were members of the ALP, which has never condoned this sort of behaviour. There is every suggestion that the Communist Party was well represented among the audience.

LETTERS IN BRIEF

No entry to the legal profession. It was quite difficult for young persons leaving school to enter the legal profession. The education of aspiring solicitors was largely done via a type of apprenticeship of about four years to a practicing solicitor. The youth thus became an "articled clerk", and was poorly paid in the first year, and his salary grew as he became more useful. There was a lot of talk currently about changing this system, and that included increasing the salary paid to him in his first year.

One retired solicitor reminded us that when he started in the profession **in 1912, he was paid nothing at all in his first year of indenture. In fact, his father actually paid the solicitor a sum of 200 Guineas to take him on.** That was a lot of money in those days. He goes on to reason that the young articled clerk is initially so useless that, without the payment of this money, it is little wonder that solicitors are reluctant to take on "articles".

Contemporary music. The ABC managed a series of very successful concerts sold under the brand of Subscription Concerts. Patrons had to pay for their tickets at the start of the year, and then take pot luck as to what was on the programme for the five concerts spread across the year.

Subscribers were complaining of the high and rising incidence of **contemporary** music in the programmes. This music was generally written since WWII, and was often considered to be **discordant and not at all harmonious**. There were many fewer performances of the works of Beethoven and Verdi, but instead pieces by **Bartok and Schoenberg. Complaints poured in.**

One writer, however, raised an interesting point. He said that when the old masters wrote their works, they were quite contemporary in their times, and that **none of them won immediate and universal acceptance**. Could not that be the case with today's contemporary music?

Stars are born not made. **Letters.** The Director of Television for the BBC enlightened us. "Your article that said that politicians are hesitant about appearing on TV is the most arrant nonsense. I often wish they were. **The truth is that you can't keep them off the screen.** Virtually every one of the 600 British politicians is convinced that he is a gifted and natural performer before the cameras. This is not necessarily so."

Censorship is not dead yet. The Council for Civil Liberties is up in arms. A man returning to Australia from overseas had a number of *Playboy* magazines confiscated at the airport by Customs officials. Playboy, as you know, always showed a photo of a nearly nude woman as the centrefold.

The Council requested permission to see the magazines in question, in company with a lawyer "aged over 50". **Customs refused the request, and did not give a reason.** The Council thinks this is an "outrageous denial of natural justice."

Teachers have enough to do? An instruction from the Stores Branch of the Public Works Department to school cleaners brought forth a few Letters from teachers

The directive said that cleaners **must not close classroom windows unless they themselves have opened them.** The teachers said that they **are supposed to teach**, but they are now required to be clerks, bankers, insurance clerks, sports coaches, and bus conductors. They asked **if cleaners' duties are to be added to their duties.**

***Stars of the past.* Letters.** Whatever happened to Bing Crosby and Frank Sinatra?

***Marbles in the schoolyard?* Letters.** I was a primary school teacher in country South Australia for forty years. Every year, in the schoolyard, we would have a cricket season and then a football season. In between, we would have a few weeks of marbles, playing a dozen different games.

Every boy, and half the girls, had an old flour bag with a cord at its neck to carry marbles. Every break-time, circles would be drawn in the sand, and the game would begin. Winners keeepers.

That brings me to my question. Where are all those marbles now? I don't believe any one would ever throw them out. So where did they go as the kids grew up. The kids don't use them in this day and age. Where did they go?

A better class of weapon. A man **armed with a broken bottle** held up the office at the railway station at Sydney's Heathcote last night. He fled with 30 Pounds. **Comment.** Nowadays robbers **are much better equipped with guns, knives and chain saws**. That is one of the benefits of advancing technology.

A famous jocket dead. **David Henry Munroe died** yesterday in Sydney Hospital. This won't mean much to most people, until they realise that this is the **Darby Monroe who was the leading jockey in the nation for years.** Among his records was the riding of **nine winners at the Sydney Cup meeting** in 1938.

Weather-proof shopping. Sydney local Councils were saying that shoppers should be protected from the weather **by awnings over shops**. Some shops had overhead protection from the rain and sun, but most **suburban shopping centres** had shops with a flat vertical front with a doorway straight into the shop....

This was no longer good enough. Moves were afoot to make shops, at their owner's expense, **provide awnings out to the kerb**, and to **create and maintain a pavement** that assured safe walking. **You can't stop progress**.

APRIL NEWS ITEMS

Mail sorters in all capital cities will start to **work to regulations** today. This means they **will not sort letters that do not have the full address written perfectly clearly.** For example, leave off the house number, or the name of the State, and your letter will pile up. They will keep the strike going for two weeks, and then review it....

They want the **automated mail sorting equipment** to be run by adult males, and not by junior girls as is proposed. Obviously, the girls would be cheaper. On the other hand, the men say they have families of five or six to support.

Cecil Scott Forester died yesterday. He was mainly known to readers as **C S Forester**, and he wrote many epics of the sea. He was famous for the Captain Horatio Hornblower series, but the very different *African Queen* was also one of his. Strangely, although his books were considered to be "naval masterpieces", **he had never been to sea.**

I must also mention writer **Evelyn Waugh who also died** a few days later. The *SMH* editorialised on him, and ended with **"there is no contemporary English writer to whom we owe more".**

The leader of the Opposition, **Arthur Calwell**, announced that if he becomes Prime Minister after the elections this year, then **he will bring all National Servicemen home from Vietnam**....

But in true Labor fashion (at the time) his Deputy leader, **Gough Whitlam**, said that if **he** was leader, he would allow each conscript **individually** to decide if he wanted to come home. If he wanted to stay, he was free to do so. Maybe the end result would be the same, but it was just another split for Labor to argue about. The Party is reported as being in **"wholesale confusion"**.

The Federal Government announced that **all National Servicemen under the age of 21** would be entitled to vote at the next election.

The CSIRO has invented new techniques that prevent the **shrinking of wool when wet**, and allows **permanent creasing that withstands wetting.** It is said to be a major boost to the **wool industry, which is under intense competition from synthetic fibres**. The new technique will eventually be known as Csiro-set**, and be a big success in rejuvenating a sluggish wool market.** Later, clothing made from **very fine wool** gradually appeared and further lifted the market for wool.

A *SMH* cartoon captured the mood in Australia. It showed a **typical Australian looking at three newspaper billboards**. One said "Rhodesian blockade latest". The second said "Vietnam riots". The third said "Conscription issue." The man's comment was **"Ho hum, better start worrying about these things again I suppose"**....

He was right. The time had come. The ferment over Vietnam was big and growing. The news media were full of it and every day, papers had at least two front-page articles on some aspect of the war. Ordinary citizens, normally apathetic, were up in arms. No one could ignore the various forms and agents of protest....

Reluctantly, we as a nation were being dragged into other people's affairs. What a nuisance.

CONCERN FOR THE ENVIRONMENT

Was the environment of much concern in 1966? **For example**, there was no Green Party, and there were only a few local Councils that had tree preservation orders. Parks and public space were constantly being alienated for the building of housing.

The answer is that there was **only a small portion of the population who had concerns, and generally only when their own immediate environment was threatened**. For example, a bowling club was to be built in a park, foreshore land was to be alienated for home units, National Forest was to be leased for grazing. Roads and cuttings were being built through nature's wonderland. Water birds, like the ibis and wild duck, were losing their breeding habitat. There was litter everywhere, at the Sydney Show, on mountain picnic areas, on railway stations.

Still, as I look back to 1956 **and** 1946, there has **now** been a big **increase in the number of Letters complaining about such matters**. Also noticeable was a small **increase in the formation of societies**, rather than individuals, for stopping the rot.

The Letters below are good examples of the protests received.

Letters, Cecil Houston. It was our turn to repay the kindness of two visiting friends from overseas, so we took them to the Sydney Easter Show. **Never have we been so ashamed and mortified**, as when we saw the amount of litter scattered around the grounds of the Show.

At 11 o'clock in the morning, the few garbage cans in evidence were chock-a-block full, so from then on the empty drink cartons, cigarette packs and food containers were dropped at random! We ate our lunch in a park amid mountains of garbage and for the rest of the afternoon, waded through the same.

Don't tell us that a huge area with thousands of sightseers can't be kept clean. At Disneyland, in California, we didn't see as much as a cigarette butt dropped without it being swept up instantly. The same applies to the Tivoli Gardens in Copenhagen and the World's Fair in New York.

Surely the Show officials could arrange a twice daily clean-up in future? If not, I'm afraid our next visit to the Sydney Easter Show will be spent with the animals in their pens – these were spotless!

Letters, Cecil Brown. Your leader of April 2 on vanishing waterbirds contains a sentence, "What could man have done to save them?" One way to help would be **to license aviculturists** who wish to be allowed to keep and breed them.

This the Fauna Protection Panel will not agree to. Are they a **protecting** panel when they give licences to gunmen for destruction of our birds, and withhold a licence from the man who likes to breed and protect them? There is abundant evidence that the aviculturist has contributed in no small way to the perpetuation of all sorts of species.

Who was responsible for breeding, from the jungle fowl of Asia, all the domestic breeds of poultry mankind now enjoys? – certainly the aviculturist, not the gunmen. The turkey of America has spread throughout the world and similarly the European goose, through the work of aviculturists. Perhaps our lyrebird could be perpetuated in the same way the aviculturist has saved many pheasant varieties from extinction.

Could not our Australian plain turkey and Cape Barren goose, etc., be preserved instead of being hastened to extinction by narrow-minded officialdom?

Say 40,000 licences to preserve and breed could tell a different story from the 40,000 licences issues for the so-called "blood sport."

Comment. A good Letter that makes its point well. Yet, was a single voice crying out. It was not the shout that developed when organised groups shout together.

OUR FRIENDS IN NEW ZEALAND

Our relations with the people and sheep across the ditch have always been pretty good. Everyone remembers the fact that we fought side by side in both World Wars, and have traded sensibly since then. If you look at the world around us, it is easy to find neighbouring nations that do not get on together, and have not done so for centuries. Japan and China come to mind. So do Russia and Poland, and even Britain and France. The easy harmony that we have with our little brothers is to be welcomed and fostered, despite their marked inferiority in many different sports.

Letters, Arthur Paterson. In reply to W Brown on old-age pensions, it must be frankly admitted that the position is just as bad as he states, and is solely brought about by the fact that the **present-day average Australian is an unimaginative, incoherent no-hoper**, quite incapable of building a nation out of the priceless heritage won for him by his forbears.

Most of the nations of Western Europe are today far ahead of Australia, and those that are not are rapidly improving their social services, even Italy and Spain, whereas Australia is rapidly drifting to the rear of the field. This is a shocking indictment of Australians who apparently are sunk in apathy, lulled by the constantly reiterated myths about prosperity and rising living standards. Australians have become so gullible and biddable that they are a sitting shot for a Communist or Fascist takeover.

I speak as a New Zealander, many years in this country and fortunately not in need of your "old-age pension."

Letters, J A Eldridge. Even though Mr Arthur Paterson dislikes us so intensely, is there any occasion for him to be so rude about it?

In his letter he describes the present-day average Australian as an unimaginative, incoherent no-hoper, and it is surprising how many other uncomplimentary terms he finds to use in his description of us. Criticism is one thing and can be accepted and forgiven even if it is ill-founded. Rudeness is another and there is never any excuse for it. But it is interesting, since he holds these views, even after living among us for so many years, that he has attained the measure of prosperity he evidently enjoys.

Fortunately, he says, he is not in need of our "old age" pension, which is what his letter is about, and he is evidently comparing it with New Zealand's age benefits which provide payments of 5 Pounds a week to elderly people without a means test. To do this, and to provide for other social service benefits that the NZ welfare State enjoys, every wage-earner is taxed 1/ in every New Zealand pound he earns, and no doubt it could be said that we should do the same here. But it has been reliably said that to remove the means test in Australia, it would cost over $260,000,000 annually, and it is safe to say that 6d in the dollar on Australian wages would not provide the money to pay for it.

Yet, without the benefits provided by New Zealand's welfare State, many New Zealanders have made Australia their home – over 60,000 of them living permanently in Sydney alone. These 60,000, including Mr Paterson, evidently prefer this country to their own despite the fact, if such it is, that we are all unimaginative, incoherent no-hopers, sunk in apathy.

Comment. Perhaps that easy harmony did not spread to **everyone** all the time. Yet I feel confident that it has persisted over the years, and happily shows no sign of vanishing.

Though, having said that, I must quote a Baron von Muhr, in New Zealand who said this week that "Australian women's complexions often resemble a well-cooked pork chop."

WHAT'S HAPPENING IN OUR CEMETERIES

Most dead people in Australia were still **buried**. This was normally in a plot in a local cemetery, alongside other family members, with a headstone. However, an increasing number were being **cremated**, though this was restricted mainly to the cities. In this case, their ashes were often placed in a wall and were marked by a plaque. **In very recent times, new lawn cemeteries were springing up.** Here, the body, or the ashes, were buried in a lawn, and a commemorative tablet was set firmly into place. This had the advantage that **the whole area can be mowed and it is relatively easy to keep very tidy**.

With that background, it is interesting to read how some old-style cemeteries were coping.

Letters, (Miss) K Campbell.   With the high cost of burial so recently in the news, perhaps now is an opportune time to write of the state of our cemeteries.

Some 14 years ago, my father died and was buried at the Northern Suburbs Catholic Cemetery and, as is customary, we purchased a family plot, no lawn cemetery being available at that time. My mother died in the later part of 1965 and was buried with my father. During these 14 years the neglect of the older part of the cemetery was nothing short of disgraceful. As the lawn cemetery has grown in size and beauty, so the older part has deteriorated.

It was pitiful, a few weeks ago, to see an elderly woman vainly trying to locate a grave among the weeds. Any time now we will witness the results of the great "burning off" of weeds in preparation for Mother's Day, with graves and headstones blackened by fire and smoke. Surely this part of the cemetery deserves the same care and respect as the new part.

The burial and headstones were all very expensive items for most of us, and I feel sure in the years to come, these old headstones will be of great interest to many. Why not maintain this older part of the cemetery so that it becomes an integral part of the new, and a place where one may visit with a certain amount of pride?

Letters, (Mrs) M Williams. I fully endorse the feeling of resentment expressed by Miss K Campbell about conditions in the older part of the Catholic section of the Northern Suburbs Cemetery.

Conditions are such that nothing less than an inspection by the responsible Minister, and the action by him that must necessarily follow, will satisfy the anger of those who have had the misfortune to inter those dear to them in this part of the cemetery.

Two weeks ago my husband attempted to reach the grave of his late mother who was interred there in 1949, but he had to abandon the attempt because the so-called path was choked by paspalum oozing with ergot and Columbian daisy weed. The whole area appears to be a breeding-ground of that weed, the seeds of which cling to the clothes of passers-by and, if it travels to our sheep country, it will be a case of heaven help the wool industry, which already has enough problems to contend with.

When the "great burn" to which Miss Campbell referred begins, our worries begin again, for on two occasions I have had to pay a monumental mason to recondition the grave of my late aunts because of fire damage.

In Brittany, where my husband owns ancestral vaults and graves, we found that they had all been damaged by shell-fire during the Liberation, but the authorities had carried out all possible structural repairs, and the paths were in perfect condition, the reason being that the cemeteries are controlled by the municipal council of the district.

I am convinced that the solution to our problems of neglected cemeteries is to eliminate all the so-called "trusts" and hand over the cemeteries to local councils now – not wait until they are closed and the funds evaporated, when the cemeteries will become a charge on local ratepayers.

One lady writes that Rookwood Cemetery is an absolute disgrace to those in charge. "I have been going there for the last 20 years and never have I seen it in such a state – up to your waist in weeds and only we know where our family graves are. Nobody else would be able to find them."

She suggests that it would be better to plough it all under, and build flats on it. Or perhaps one of the new car parks that are eating up the land. "Anything would be more useful than the jungle we now have."

Comment. Sadly, there were other Letters round the nation that said the same thing. It seems to have been a national problem.

There were good reasons why some people at this time preferred the burgeoning lawn cemeteries. Given the state of the older ones, it was not surprising that they then grew so quickly in popularity.

VIETNAM NEWS

There is so much news and commentary on Vietnam that I could fill book after book keeping you up to date. I cannot spare that space. So, **from here**, you can assume that the demos and arguments, and what-have-you, are going on all the time, but I will only report **new ideas and events**. That way I might be able to keep you informed in less than two pages a month.

These Letters add **new ideas and slants on the news**.

Letters, S M Outerbridge. Defence of democracy seems to be the only justification for sending troops to Vietnam at all – either volunteers or conscripts.

We are not at war with any country, nor is any other country threatening our safety.

Neither is the United States at war with any country: no country is threatening its safety.

The US is at war in support of the idea that somewhere, in Asia, sometime, in the nebulous future, any form of government other than a democracy, may pose a threat to the free world.

So America appoints itself the arbiter of what form of government these countries shall have and, in doing so, reduces them to such a shambles that they have very little chance of formulating any form of government at all.

I don't know what the terms of enlistment are for our volunteer army, but I doubt if any single member thought they would be used anywhere, any time, in support of any other nation which decided that somewhere, in some remote part of the world, democracy was threatened.

I imagine that they enlisted with the highest of motives – that they would be in the service of Australia and its territories if they were threatened with aggression, **not with the idea of stamping out rebellions by races who resented the invasion of their countries by democracy.**

Letters, A Cameron. The statement by the Anglican Dean of Melbourne (the Very Rev T W Thomas) that **his church had not adopted any policy on the war** in Vietnam made appalling reading.

This is particularly so, as from day to day we are told by the Australian Government of the dire perils that await us!

Leo Tolstoy's thought-provoking play *War and Peace* has yet some 10 days to run in Melbourne, and I would urge the Dean to see it. He would be reminded that millions of lives were lost in the First World War, with millions more in the Second World War.

This surely proves the futility of all wars, when even the victors seemingly came off second best.

If still unable to reconcile their private thoughts with Christian principles, church leaders might well demand that all up and coming young politicians so desirous of sending others off to war, be the first to man the barricades. The result would be interesting.

Letters, Adrian Beks. Lieut-Colonel R K Wilson states that religious and conscientious objection to military service stems basically from fear and moral or physical cowardice.

During the last war an Austrian peasant, Franz Jagerstatter, suffered a brutal death at the hands of the Nazis because of his refusal on conscientious grounds to obey orders.

Jagerstatter had to be killed, of course, as his "cowardice" might have spread and adversely affected the patriotic fervour and heroism of those engaged in herding women and children into the gas chambers of Treblinka and Auschwitz.

We should never forget the fact that without the kind of blind obedience which Colonel Wilson advocates, the indescribable atrocities committed by the followers of Hitler and Stalin would not have been possible.

LETTERS IN BRIEF

Oyster-eating orgy.   Every year in Sydney, the industry likes to have an event where mountains of seafood are eaten. The main draw card is the oyster-eating competition when contestants are invited to eat as many oysters as they can in about ten minutes.

One lady complained against all this gluttony and vulgarity. She watched as 675 contestants ate 2,600 dozens of oysters, together with huge amounts of prawns and crayfish, and all of it washed down with beer and stout. She went on to tell us that this is giving the State of NSW a very bad image interstate and also overseas.

Another writer replied that he had no statistics on who participated, but he did know that the first two place-getters were from Queensland and Perth, and the third was from Colorado in the US. This suggested to him that the image the State is sending is one of fun and flavour. He said he attends every year, and would still do so if it were in Colorado or anywhere in the world.

Reciprocal driving licences. **Letters.** Complaints pointed out that a person who holds a driving licence from NSW cannot drive in Victoria. And vice versa. And for the other States. This was important for people on driving holidays. They said that all States asked a lot of questions about distances. For example, at what distance did you have to dip your lights.

The trouble was that these distances varied in the different States. This made it extra hard to get a licence in any other State.

The SMH is in luke-warm water. **The clergy have been in the news lately for its split views on the Vietnam war.** The *SMH* published an article by one of its journalists that **listed the WWII record of Australia's bishops**. Some had served in the Armed Services, and some had not. Some readers saw the article as implying **that these men, now Bishops, were not competent to express opinions** because of their war-time experience, whether in the Services or not.

Correspondents challenged the logic of this assumption and also the completeness of the article. They said that some clergy were medically unfit to go to war, and that in some cases their Bishops could not spare them, and in other cases they performed vital roles within Australia. But, they said, it was **wrong to assume current opinions reflected their war records**....

The Herald got close to apologising. "No criticism of those bishops without war records was intended...." nor was there any implication that the padres' current judgement was faulty.

Improved betting service. **Letters.** The old days of the SP bookie up the lane behind the pub had gone, and all States were reaping big money from the TAB shops. One punter was full of praise for all aspects of TAB services, except that recently **he had placed a bet in Eucla**, and had then driven to his home town of Esperance. But then he found that to collect his winnings, **he had to go back to Eucla.** He called for a system **allowing collections at any agency within the State. Or even nationwide.**

P-plates still have problems. **Letters.** The authorities are talking about **introducing provisional licences for young drivers** for a period after they go off their L-plates. I find that as I drive with my son, a learner driver, there are many other drivers who do not respect the plates, and who crowd him, and cut him off when he slows them up.

It seems to me that they will do the same for P-platers too. The problem will not go away. In fact, it will just go on for longer with perhaps even more impatience. The problem is not the P-platers. It is the other cranky drivers who can't wait a few seconds.

The Pill on the march. I said earlier that the new Pill was giving women a lot more choices than they had previously had. But there was much opposition to it. This came mainly from the Churches, especially the Catholic Church, which had long advocated the rhythm method of gambling on pregnancy. All sorts of moral arguments were raised, and all sorts of scare stories were told, but women gradually, slowly but surely, came to grips with the various arguments, as the usage of the pill increased.

Trouble in the Courts. A Sydney Supreme Court trial **for murder** was disrupted when **all four witnesses for the Crown failed to appear**. The four women had appeared at an earlier hearing. Now they had disappeared from their homes. The trial proceeded, but the **charge had to be reduced to manslaughter**. Intimidation is feared.

MAY NEWS ITEMS

A new super grade petrol, with a higher octane rating, will be on sale next week. It will cost 97 cents per gallon, compared to the present price of 87 cents.

Here's **a good slogan from a recent demo**. *"Our Conscripts to Relace South Vietnam Deserters."* **It may or may not be true**, but it packed a punch.

Warrnambool racetrack in Melbourne usually ran two steeplechase or hurdle races on its programme. These two events were somewhat different, but both involved the horse **jumping over hurdles**, and sometimes water hazards. They were usually longer than other horse races, and the exhaustion rate and the many falls made them popular with punters....

On Saturday, the apparent winner of such an event **slowed down after the race**, only to find that the other horses kept racing and came past him. It turned out that the **winning post for steeplechases was different from normal races**, and was poorly marked. **So he started to pull up a half furlong too soon**. The jockey, new to the track, was fined $200.

After the annual Commemoration Day at Sydney Uni, **1,000 students protested** at Wynyard rail station **against the new bogey: automation.** It was widely feared that **machines would take over the jobs of people**.

The US is urging the United Nations to **draw up treaties that will protect the moon** and other planets **from exploitation** by any one country. For example, no country would be able to claim ownership of all or any part of the moon, or any other body in outer space.....

It assumes that **humans can one day visit outer space**, and the moon. **You can believe me that this is beyond the technical reach of mankind, and it is foreign to all concepts of any religion, and the whole idea is laughable. Forget it.   It will never happen.**

Governments in all States are considering making records available that would allow the **setting up of agencies to create records** of those who defaulted on debts. Here was **the birth of the credit checks** so much used 50 years later.

China reminded the world today that it **is a potent force** by exploding its **third atom bomb**. It was estimated to be 130 Kilotons, whereas the first two were each about 20 Kilotonnes.

Residents of the suburb of North Sydney are up in arms. They are just across the Sydney Harbour from Sydney city, and have seen parking meters installed there. This was not at all a popular move....

Now**, the local Council of this low-rise suburb is proposing to install parking meters** in the shopping centre at North Sydney. Residents are outraged. So too are suburban dwellers in all Sydney suburbs. What if the idea spread that **revenue could be raised** anywhere in Sydney?....

Don't worry about it. North Sydney was assured that the move was only to ration parking spaces evenly during the day. **It certainly was not designed with the idea of raising money. Perish the thought.**

NEWS AND VIEWS ON VIETNAM

Enter the Buddhist monks. Buddhist monks in Vietnam are very numerous, and despite their image of piety, are in fact **a strident and militant group that wants the government ousted**, and free elections to be held in the region. In Danang, Vietnam's second largest city, **the Buddhist monks** proliferate, and **claim the government wishes to assassinate them all**. They are staging military attacks on Vietnamese troops there, and are close to taking control. As early as last week in Danang, five pagodas, where monks were holding out, **were attacked by government troops**. In a week's fighting, **200 Buddhists were killed, and hundreds were injured.**

A Red union takes a stand. Meanwhile, here in Australia, **the Seamens' Union had refused to man a supply ship**, the *Boonaroo,* which was headed **for our troops in Vietnam**. This was because the Union, Red-controlled, was opposed to Australia's involvement in the fracas. **The Union was pitted against the Government and wide-spread public opinion.** In backing down, it saved face by saying that **the ship could be manned by volunteer seamen** willing to carry the materials to our troops.

Letters, T J Beaumont. I view with alarm the remarks of the Communist General Secretary of the Seamen's Union, which is "opposed to manning a ship involved in the Vietnam war".

Whether one supports the Government's policy on Vietnam or not, it is a fact that there is a contingent of Australian armed forces in South Vietnam which has earned respect from the Vietnamese and Americans, and has thus brought credit to Australia.

The Government should decide **whether it is an act of treason or not.**

It is interesting to refer to *The Seamen's Journal* of March, 1952, where Mr Elliott proudly boasts, "At the outbreak of the war in Korea, seamen stopped work in all Australian ports, held meetings and decided not to take ships with troops or war supplies from Australia."

It is a sad day for Australia when such an organisation can be the final arbiter on the question of whether we should ship supplies to our troops.

Club's aid to Regiment. This device below is a novel way of giving support to our overseas troops.

Letters, R Cubis, Commanding Officer, Holsworthy. I would be grateful for the opportunity to bring to public attention an action by a group of kind-hearted citizens of Sydney, designed to assist and encourage members of the Regular Army who will be serving in South Vietnam soon.

The Muirfield Golf Club, a private golf club whose links are at North Rocks, near Parramatta, has decided to take under its wing, as an individual project, a Regular Army unit serving overseas. The club has chosen 1st Field Regiment, Royal Regiment of Australian Artillery. The club is devoting time and effort to support this regiment in both a tangible and intangible manner.

The club has already purchased sporting goods, which have been gratefully received by the regiment, and has undertaken to maintain a supply of similar equipment.

This material support is of great assistance to the regiment; but the moral support is, perhaps, of even greater importance and is a tremendous comfort to our soldiers.

Conscription of British. A 20-year-old migrant points out that he is liable for the lottery and then a call-up, just because he is a Britisher. He complains on three fronts. **Firstly**, Greeks and Italians, and **lads from other nations, are safe from call-up**.

Secondly, that if an **Australian young man** was resident in England and was conscripted **to fight in Poland or Greece**, the Australian Government and its people would be outraged.

Thirdly, Australian migration officials, recruiting in London, **pointedly ignore questions about conscription**, and quickly move on almost begging Poms to come out here.

His Letter ends with the statement that he was one of the lucky ones whose birthday went into the lottery but did not come out.

Comment. These are all good points. The following Letter tries to answer one of them.

Letters, Howard Toon. A Webster misses the vital point in his letter. The very reason that young British migrants are quite properly liable for military service is because they are **British** subjects. They do not belong to a minority group. All native born people of the British Isles, Australia, New Zealand or Canada are British, and if they come to live in this country they should be prepared to help defend it.

The question of whether or not the "numerous Greeks, Italians, etc.," should be called up for National Service is a different argument entirely, as these people are not British. This is not to regard them in any derogatory way, but their responsibility is different and their loyalty could quite possibly follow different ideas from ours.

I do not know upon what grounds Mr Webster was granted his indefinite deferment, but, as an Englishman, I feel disgusted that he considers himself one of the "lucky" ones. He would do better to feel sorry that he is not performing his natural duty.

SONG AND DANCE ROUTINES

Eisteddfods were still an important part of the Australian cultural scene in Australia in the 1960's. Every city and large municipality held an annual event that gave people of all ages a chance to publicly compete in events that showed their ability in some form of cultural activity. Children aged six might dance, boys aged 10 might do elocution, 13-year-old girls might play the piano, adult males might form a choir, women might trill as sopranos or inspire terror as contraltos. There was something for every one. At the end of each event, a small inscribed silver cup was given to the winner, who felt justifiably proud.

Still, a Welsh lady wrote that the programme was not quite complete. **She advised that eisteddfods originated in Wales, where the emphasis was "on bardic talent."** She wanted the emphasis to be on **the writing of poetry**. "Epics, lyrics, a verse-play, a ballad. Why make a travesty of the original Welsh idea, which goes so far back in history?"

Comment. This brought forth the following response, full of history, that explained quite a lot.

Letters, M Gunn, Organising Sec, City of Sydney Eisteddfod. In the early days of the national Welsh eisteddfod in the fourteenth century, when they were irregularly held, the only means of livelihood, for bards and minstrels, were obtainable from royal or noble households or in public competitions, and they were duly honoured. Printing, radio, filming and television had not then been invented.

Even the Royal National Welsh Eisteddfod has changed, and I have not been able to trace **harp** contests in various copies of the Welsh National Eisteddfod publications, although the harp ranked next to the bard in importance, and still remains in the public mind the emblem of the eisteddfod.

May I add that Mrs Anders' reading of our 1964 syllabus appears to have been superficial? She alleges that the noble eisteddfod has been turned into a "song and dance affair." Actually out of a total of 474 contests in our 1964-65 syllabus, only 12 sections were devoted to such events, while 86 were devoted to forms of speech, 188 to vocal or instrumental performances of music, involving close study of the works of masters, and bringing international fame to such past competitors as Joan Sutherland, Ron Grainer, Kathleen Gorham and many others.

THE DECLINE IN BIRTHRATE

The Government was always lamenting the decline in birth rate. It wanted our young men and women to breed and have lots of kids, so that our Asian neighbours would be so impressed by the size of our population that they would not attack us. Given that these same Asian nations had populations ranging from ten- to one hundred-times bigger than ours, it seems we might have needed to devote every second of every day to multiplying.

Still, with the motto of "Populate or Perish", we were intently debating why our birthrate was falling. Among many theories, only some of them sensible, this Letter below offers basic advice.

Letters, (Mrs) S Cowie. Our Governments say they cannot understand Australia's falling birthrate. It is easier to blame the pill, and accuse young married women of being too materialistic, than to be honest enough to admit that land, houses and the cost of living are completely out of proportion to an ordinary working man's wage.

We have been married for two years and have just completed payments on a block of land, which we were saving for a long time before our marriage. Now we are saving for a fairly large sum of money to pay for plans, councils costs, fences, etc., and balance between the cost of a house and the amount of money we can borrow. That's not to mention furniture! We would dearly love a family but a baby cannot sleep on the floor, or live on fresh air. And before we could have a family, we would have to save some money for hospital fees, prams, cots, etc.

Believe me, I would much rather stay home and have a family than go to work each day, but I know you cannot house a family in a small two-roomed flat.

In a country as big as this, land and homes should never have been allowed to be so highly priced.

BRITAIN AND EUROPE

Talks were continuing between Britain on the one hand, and Europe on the second hand, and the Empire on the third hand. The Brits were keen to join with European nations to form a common market and, no matter what we said, that would mean the end to the preference that we now enjoyed in selling to Britain. As we all know, that eventually happened, and Australia had to find new markets for its products. Which it did.

In the meantime, however, the prospect of Britain cutting off its buying was most disturbing, so talks were going on all over the place about what might happen. The Letter below gives one small glimpse of what important people were talking about. I suggest **you do not try to come to grips with**

the details, just accept the Letter as a sample of the issue and worries under discussion worldwide.

Letters, C D Kemp, Director, Institute of Public Affairs, Melbourne. Your editorial suggests that Sir Alexander Downer's statements in London last week on the Common Market represent the Australian viewpoint. I find it hard to believe that this is so.

The unmistakable implication of what Sir Alexander Downer was reported to have said in London was that Australia is opposed to Britain's entry into the Market. I doubt whether this correctly represents Australian opinion today.

It is much clearer now even than it was four years ago (when Britain first applied for entry) that British membership of the Market is inevitable.

That this would be a great historic step forward for Britain, for Europe, and for the world can hardly be gainsaid. With Britain as a part of Europe, Sir Winston Churchill's great vision of a United States of Europe with all that it means for the stability and security of the world could become an attainable goal.

If Britain were to enter the Market, Australia would be right to press for the best possible deal for her primary products, but the great issues at stake far outweigh any parochial considerations of narrow self-interest.

It would be unfortunate if unattractive doctrines of "Little Australianism," of the kind voiced by Sir Alexander Downer, were to gain any hold over Australian attitudes.

These doctrines have already been evident in the hostile approach of some to the import of overseas capital, which is so indispensable to rapid development of the Australian continent.

Such attitudes would be even more dangerously short-sighted and reprehensible if they result in Australian opposition to the great political regrouping which is now slowly and painfully taking shape in Western Europe, the seed-bed of two disastrous world wars in our lifetime.

HAPPY MOTHERS' DAY

The Rev Jones at the Lane Cove Congregational Church decided to brighten the lives of mothers on the special day by giving them a blast from the pulpit. He said that many mothers were giddy gossiping gadabouts, they spent too much time in the beauty parlour or at the bridge table. Warming up, he accused them of blowing cigarette smoke in their babies' eyes, and keeping them awake with numerous noisy cocktail parties or boozy dinners.

"Like the prophet, I want to charge this type of motherhood with cruelty." He went on to say that 60 per cent of the needs of children were being neglected in Australian homes, and many children were being reared in paganism.

This was not what mothers wanted to hear on Mothers Day. So a number of them sent in rejoinders.

Letters, Judy Olding. It only requires half a mind and an average physical capacity to run a modern house. During school hours, these amoral fiends can therefore play golf, tennis, bridge, have their hair done, attend a morning session at a cinema, enrol in a class, go out to lunch, and even reach the dizzy heights of sophistication to do charity or club work.

They are not usually being "unfaithful to their marriage vows," which sounds much more interesting anyway, nor are they practising "cruelty by neglect."

What would Mr Jones like his women to be doing? Sitting brooding about little Jimmy's coming exams? Assiduously tatting anti-frost plant covers? Or spending the entire day cooking huge meals to accelerate her husband's coronary prospects?

Certainly the development of the young is important – but within reason. The most fortunate children have mothers who are professional or business women, from choice. They are identities – not just Joe Blow's wife, or Jim's mum. They are not obsessed with domestic trivia, and can give sound adult advice when asked. They are well organised and can afford assistance to balance the time away from home.

But there were others who agreed, at least in part.

Letters, (Mrs) Pamela M Newton. It surely is a brave man to hurl such bullets at womanhood on Mother's Day or any other day, and without a doubt we are all guilty in varying degrees. Once married, so many become bored with caring for husband, children and the home, then the trend is for someone to come in and take over, or deposit the children in city boarding schools so that mother is almost as free as a bird.

If one **does** enjoy family life at home with all its work and responsibilities, I have heard the remark, "Poor thing, she's in a rut!"

Family life is the most important structure of society and yet is so constantly abused by mothers who have not their children's interest at heart.

Comment. I suspect that admonitions delivered from the pulpit, on a celebratory day, do more harm that good. Even if you agree that the women in question were doing harm. It might have been better had Rev Jones picked his moment more judiciously.

LETTERS IN BRIEF

Vive la France. The French Government has announced its intention to conduct a series of atom bomb tests in the

Pacific, and expects them to go on last for at least five years. It claims that the fall-out will do no harm at all because the atomic cloud will drift in certain directions to places that have no habitation. The world **raised a sceptical eyebrow over this claim**. But no **major power will seriously try to stop the tests** because they themselves have been doing the same thing.

Objections have appeared in all Australian newspapers, and of course have not changed anything. The only response that **they** elicited was a charming note from a Frenchman that said that France was a great power and had every right to do things to keep that power. Not only that, she also **had the right to keep her colonies**, despite world pressure to vacate them.

He was happy that the upstart governments of Australia and New Zealand were not able to frustrate the French plans. He went on to say that the French flag will continue to fly over France's Pacific possessions long **after Australia and New Zealand have crumbled to nothing**.

Comment. This Letter was so inflammatory that I suspect it was a leg-pull. **What do you think?**

Retaining migrants. The Federal government was concerned that so **many British migrants to this nation were returning home**. Many of them came by assisted passage, and this cost Australia quite an amount of money, and then this was wasted when the Brits went away.

The problem according to one writer was that many of them **came out with the intention of staying only the minimum of two years**, and after a working holiday for that time, packing up and going back to the ole Blighty.

Comment. The writer was undoubtedly correct. But our Government was "unconcerned". It took the attitude that this nation was so attractive that a big percentage of those who came with this attitude actually stayed on. Overall, the odds were that the wastage would be more than covered by the stayers.

More on returning migrants. One migrant, dissatisfied with Australia, explained why he had left these fair shores. He said that Australians demanded too much of migrants in that they want them to **change their customs and ways overnight. They are largely intolerant**, absorbed by sport, women and beer, with a high level of intolerance based on ignorance.

I would not like the task of arguing that this writer was wrong. But, needless to say, a few other writers sprang to our defence.

Letters, Robert Wilson. Your writer set out most clearly why the English migrant returns to his homeland.

My grandfather might well have written in the same terms. He arrived in Australia in the 1850s, made a modest fortune, reared a family, returned to Scotland 10 times and found it an impossibility to find one good word for Australia. He died here, however, after finally settling down for the last 20 years of life in the country that he found so lacking in the Scottish way of life.

I'm afraid Mr Wilkinson had better return to his own country. Our lack of culture and English ways and customs may well be remedied in the misty future, but I guess that Mr Wilkinson (like my grandfather) won't be on hand to enjoy the benefits.

In the meantime I'll settle for Aussie sunshine and beer, its sport, and, speaking personally, my wife and daughters just suit me fine.

Cuisine on Sundays. **Letters.** Every Sunday we end up at a barbi. Every Sunday, I am told a number of times that you should drink white wine with fish, and red wine with steak. That is part of the Sunday barbi ritual.

I drink rose. In case you do not know, that is sort of half way between. What should I eat with it? If I get it wrong, the smart alecs will tell me again that I can't enjoy my food unless I get the match-up right. Is`there some sort of animal half-way between a whiting and a bull that I can eat? Then what?

Get on the hospital Board. **Letters.** In Victorian hospitals, it only takes a donation of two dollars to turn a donor into a contributor. Then, that person is eligible to stand for a position on the committee. It is recommended that more persons do that, rather than criticising the work of others. That should increase the performance of Boards, and reduce the large number of hospitals in the red.

Other writers were quick to point out that most organisations are similarly open to the man in the street getting involved. Most of them said this was a good thing. Yet one intrepid writer said that the man in the street should stay in the street, and leave running enterprises to his betters.

The price of fame. **At a concert** with a crowd of 1,500, at Sydney Town Hall, **singer Normie Rowe** was trapped on stage by a group of 200 screaming girls. They bustled him, and **he fell 10 feet off the stage, and was knocked unconscious**. He was trodden on and kicked in the face and body. Police eventually reached him, and he **was taken by ambulance to a hospital**. He suffered no permanent injury, and **was released about five hours later**.

JUNE NEWS ITEMS

Over the last month, **Indonesia and Malaya have suddenly started to talk sensibly** to each other about their difficulties. **They have now stopped fighting**, their troops and guerillas have been withdrawn, and peace is the order of the day....

As a result, **most Australian troops "will soon leave"** Malaya and Borneo. Those remaining will be used only to fight off "foreign aggression", whatever that might be.

Comment. Let us all **hope that the peace arrangements being made will stand the test of time.**

Danish-born Jorn Utzon, speaking in Copenhagen, said he "found it **surprising that the NSW Government could complete the Opera House without him."** He was **prepared to return to his old job, provided** there was no further outside interference....

Meanwhile, in Sydney**, changes to Utzon's plan for the main hall** seemed likely because of perceived failures in Utzon's plans for seating arrangements. **The war of words continues.**

16 Australian persons received **knighthoods from the Queen** this weekend. They included **artist William Dobell.**

On the Queen's Birthday weekend, cities and towns round Australia are generally made hideous by **the barrage of crackers**. Last night, Sydney and much of the coast of NSW was spared this because of steady rain....

But residents should not rejoice yet. The crackers were no doubt not dampened, so they will certainly be used in the future.

The Federal Court of Appeals decided that **rents on properties**, built before 1954 and permanently occupied, **should be decided having due regard** for factors such as current cost of living and inflation over the years. This **should** have meant that **rent control would be abolished**....

The background is that the rents paid for such properties had been **fixed at 1941 levels. What a bonanza for the renters. What a swindle for the land lords.** All State Governments had refused to bring these rents up to date because of the **electoral back-lash from renters** if they did....

The Court of Appeal's decision said that rents should now be increased. The NSW State Government (and others) immediately said "there will be no general increase in rents. **We will have to find ways of preventing this from happening". Talk about being lost in a time warp!**

A crowd of 56,000 Rugby League fans turned out to watch Balmain play St George at the Sydney Cricket Ground. This was not a Final, just **an ordinary club match.**

Police in NSW and others States are now routinely using, for the first time, **officers in plain clothes and in unmarked cars** for their road patrols.

NEWS AND VIEWS FROM VIETNAM

Sydney march of veterans. **June 8th. 500 troops marched through the streets of Sydney. They were soldiers returning from one year's** service in Vietnam. **They were given a polite reception**, and only a few protesters were reported....

There had been fears that crowds of demonstrators would mar the march. However, it was clear that the 200,000 people lining the route thought **the fighting men deserved the applause, even though some hated the cause they were fighting for. There were no Nashos among the marchers.**

Death toll. **The number of Australians killed so far in Vietnam is 26.** Also, 149 have been wounded and incapacitated....

Two of the dead were conscripted National Servicemen. They were aged 19 and 20 years.

Labor leader Arthur Calwell is trying to persuade more people to vote for him in the elections at the end of this year. He is now **promising to bring home the Nashos from Vietnam by Christmas if he is elected. Whether voters will believe in him remains to be seen.**

Trading with the enemy? The Australian Wheat Board has negotiated the sale of 600,000 tons of wheat to Communist China for a sum of 30 million dollars. Given the state of play in Vietnam, and that China is backing the Viet Cong, this sale will be questioned.

Air attack on North Vietnam. June 30th. 46 US planes from an aircraft carrier bombed oilfields on the outskirts of Hanoi, the capital of North Vietnam. **This is the first air attack on the North.** A second attack followed the next day....

The attacks, authorised by President Johnson, were **heavily criticised world-wide**....

Our Prime Minister, Harold Holt, in Washington told Johnson that he was deeply relieved that Johnson had "**the firmness of resolution, the clarity of recognition** which ensured the **continued, uninterrupted effort; indeed, an accelerated and augmented effort in this field**"....

He then uttered the words for which he is famous. "All the way with L B J"....

Guess what the North will now do after the bombings?

A tough night at a meeting. **June 22ⁿᵈ.** Tonight, the **Leader of the Opposition, Arthur Calwell**, had spoken at a political meeting in the Mosman Town Hall. He was speaking against conscription, and the meeting was attended by 800 people. When the meeting ended, he spent some minutes talking to well-wishers on the pavement, then he got into his car....

At this point, a 22-year-old man emerged from the small remaining crowd, advanced to the car and **fired a .22 rifle though the window, apparently intending to kill Calwell**....

The bullet missed him, but the window shattered and Calwell's face was badly cut by flying glass. The assailant was captured by two youths after a short chase. Calwell, following a close shave with death, was taken to North Shore Hospital, where it was found that the cuts to his face were the only injuries he sustained. He was, however, badly shaken, and was kept in the hospital overnight....

Police as yet have not suggested any reason for the attempted murder. It was reported, and I happen to know it is true, that the youth was initially charged with **"Firing a rifle at Arthur Calwell and missing**." The charge was soon amended to a more suitable version.

ROLLER GAMES

Some readers will remember the number of TV programmes that showed people on roller skates racing round tracks and trying to mangle other competitors. Or perhaps people on roller skates playing on fields like ice hockey rinks, and trying to do the same thing. These shows all came from the USA, and had names like *Roller Derby*, *Roller Bladers* or the *Skating Game*. In any case, violence was their theme, rules were just a joke, and the show was a flop if someone was not maimed or shamed.

Letters, Thelma F Bate. During a period of recovery, I have had the opportunity of watching television sessions that I would not normally see, among them the "Roller Games" sessions. I can only assume that very few non-teenage people watch these sessions, otherwise there must surely have been a storm of protest long before this.

Is there no supervision at all over the type of spectacle that can be presented as entertainment? Is near-nudity the only aspect of public presentations that calls forth protest? Does the cult of "freedom of expression" and "natural living" mean that we have to return to the jungle?

I have never before seen organised brutality and violence presented so openly. Two men fighting in a boxing ring present a sissy performance compared with the roller "game" that I watched one Saturday afternoon. One of the most shocking aspects is, of course, that the teams are mixed youths and girls, and there is not only vicious violence between men, and between women, but also between men and women.

The stadium was packed with screaming teenagers from 12 years old, howling their encouragement to the teams in this organised exhibition of gang violence.

While teenagers, still in the susceptible years during which their life pattern is determined, are being subjected to unhealthy excitement of this type, what hope have parents or teachers, or youth clubs, in their attempts to train youth to accept the discipline of decent standards of living or the responsibilities of citizenship?

Russia and China must surely be quietly smiling as they watch the Western countries engaged in steadily destroying the very qualities in their way of life on which their strength was built.

May I present my shocked protests at the importation of roller "games" as a public entertainment?

Comment. Other writers had the same idea. One mother objected as well to **the enthusiasm of the commentator** as he relates how one girl has sworn to destroy another. He then goes on, in **a voice of hysterical excitement**, to wonder if she can make good her threat. Then, he prattles on assuring us that they are all good sports. This is apparently essential for the **wholesome image of the game**.

Another mother watched the show just once. She saw a girl who had been knocked over and was semi-conscious. Four other girls "politely jumped on top of her head." She says that thank goodness her 15-year-old-son does not care to watch it. She counts herself lucky for this.

Comment. Still, there is no doubt that shows with violence and intimidation do rate well on TV. Rugby League for years has had many good rules, and increasing protection for players. Yet it is the big hits that people "ooh" at, and talk about. Ice hockey has a devoted following, but is just the roller game on ice. Wrestling and boxing have attracted multitudes of viewers over the years. I suspect that, no matter how much some of us might tut-tut, violence and sadism on TV are here to stay.

AN UNINTENDED CONSEQUENCE

Education authorities across the nation were having a wonderful time. All States were considering making changes to the way their schools function, right from Kinder up to university level. In NSW, the Wyndham Report was soon to be implemented, and among the changes there, was the increase in High School years from five to six. This meant that from next year, extra numbers of pupils will have to be accommodated, and somehow an increase in classroom space will have to be found. This coming change had been visible for years, so in most cases the consequences had been thought out and planned for. But a few small details slipped past the policy makers. Here is one of them.

Letters, T V Thiele. Despite the recently announced additional expenditure ("crash program"), the side effects of the lack of accommodation in existing High Schools next year will be large in number, and far reaching in the manner in which they affect schools and children. I would draw your attention to one of these problems.

My son attends Fort Street Boys' High School and he is an enthusiastic member of the school choir. The school choir at Fort Street has a membership of 130 boys who perform adult music with a skill and enthusiasm which is unique in a boys' school in this State. The choir has an illustrious record of achievements in eisteddfod, broadcasting, television, recording and appearances with the Sydney Symphony Orchestra, and is fortunate in having as its choirmaster a person who must rank as a leader in his field in Australia.

Such a group depends entirely upon the first form boys' unchanged voices for its soprano line. As plans stand at present, Fort Street will **have no first form boys** housed at the school next year – the choirmaster assures me that this will mean the end of the fine choral tradition which he and the boys, working before and after school, have maintained for many years.

Here is a case where lack of buildings will create a problem which might never be solved. One hundred and thirty boys will be without what is, for them, one of the most meaningful aspects of their school life. And what of these first form boys next year? There will be no opportunity for them to enjoy the benefits of this fine choral tradition. How many years will it take to undo the damage of one year?

PAYMENT OF COUNCILLORS

Local Councils round the nation were run by decision-making bodies of elected people from all walks of life. These people were motivated by public spirit, or by problems with particular issues, or by personal aims such as greed. They often did a good job, and sometimes they did not. But until now, they were not paid, other than out-of-pocket expenses.

Under new proposals that were creeping round the nation, some Councils were paying Councillors a small emolument for their services, and also perhaps an **allowanc**e for expenses that they might or might not actually incur. In all, the payments involved were insignificant, and would not visibly impact the budget at all.

Still, tempers were being raised by the issue as a few Letters will demonstrate.

In the first, long, Letter, a Councillor from Bunbury in Western Australia argues that the sum to be paid is of

little consequence for a businessman who is already well catered for. He claims that the sum also means nothing to an employee who is docked for his time spent in attending to Council matters. This latter person is so devoted that he willingly makes the sacrifice

He goes on to say that any such expenditure by Councillors should be seen in the context of their **controlling huge revenue collectively round Australia**. Company Directors, who spend a lot less, are paid infinitely more.

Comment. Of course it is true that most Councillors are properly motivated by civic concern. Most of them do the best they can. But, there are some conspicuous Councils that have over the years been seen to be self-serving, for example, in handling developments in real estate. There have been others that have fallen under the control of some particular political Party, and who have administered more in the interests of their own Party rather than the local community.

Coming back to 1966, it was clear that the idea of small payments was supported by most voters. But that did not mean that most of them thought that all Councillors were all well-meaning saints. They did not think thus, and cynicism of Councillors' role was widespread.

Some element of this comes out in the Letter below.

Letters, Arthur R Jobson. Aspirants for civic office know, or should know, that certain and inevitable inroads will be made on their time, both in an out of business hours. This applies equally to any avenue of community service undertaken. Being aware of this, therefore, it is significant that at each triennial election for local government office, there is usually a long list of candidates eager for the honour of civic representation. Ratepayers and residents are literally bombarded with advertising matter promising that with the election of so-and-so their municipality will become a veritable showpiece, that the wishes of the local residents will be paramount, and so on, ad lib.

But experience has shown that in far too many cases, the goods do not come up to the label. Scarcely a week passes without some protest being made against decisions of councils which run contrary to the wishes of the people. Or they are in direct contrast to what would seem sound civic forethought and planning.

Reviewing the sorry list, one is led to consider that rather than argue the pros and cons of **payment** to local government representatives, **there should be a more strict control exercised over the operations of such groups**. It was understood that the State Planning Authority would in some degree perform this function, but no indication has been forthcoming that this organisation is displaying any authority or, if it comes to that, any planning.

In the meantime, the unplanned jumble that passes for progress in Sydney continues despite the protests of interested and responsible citizens.

Comment. The above writer was very moderate. He only **suggested** that Councils were often not as good as they might be. He was kind not to press the point.

UNDERGROUND POWER CABLES

In 1956, there was no talk at all about power cables being placed underground. It was just taken for granted that telegraph poles with their yardarms and loopy wires would bring us all of our electricity.

Since then, our budding small army of environmentalists has put the underground laying of cables on their various lists. They were mainly influenced by examples from the USA, where a number of new estates had been established with this feature.

So by 1966, it was appearing on the agenda of public debate. No one here had much real information on the pros and cons, but the various sides to the argument were lining up.

Letters, J Bartholomew. While I must agree that untidiness and a general lack of civic pride should be abhorred, I find very little objection to power poles and other similar objects of road furniture.

No one (other than perhaps an engineer) would regard a power line as a pretty sight. But it can hardly be regarded as untidy, dirty or unpleasant either. And when one considers that the placing of these lines underground would cost (if reports are correct) up to five to six times normal construction, with the possibility of adding to delays in restoring supply in times of emergency, etc., it must surely be a subject of some conjecture as to whether it is worthwhile.

Worst of all, if the placing of power lines underground is going to mean that orderly looking poles are to be replaced by miles and miles of constant road openings and excavations, then I can find no aesthetic satisfaction in the suggestion whatever, to say nothing of the possibility of higher electricity charges and inconvenience to motor traffic, etc.

Letters, Donald Gazzard. It will no doubt be a long time before all poles are removed and wires put underground in all existing areas. But this is no reason why past practices and mistakes should be repeated in every new suburb and subdivision as they are built.

Underground reticulation is now standard practice in residential areas in the USA, where it is a normal requirement in obtaining a building loan. One reason is the reduced maintenance necessary.

Because of lack of Australian experience, underground reticulation costs have in the past been exaggerated (the "up to five or six times normal" quoted). However, one Sydney suburban development has now been fully reticulated with low-voltage underground supply and very detailed cost figures of the actual installation are available which give realistic comparisons with overhead costs.

In real money (even including for the underground connections to the houses) the extra cost was not more than $80 per house, and there are indications that the cost of the cable may soon be reduced, making the difference even less. This figure bears out US experience.

The proliferation of poles and overhead wires, and the consequent lopping of trees, on our streets are major contributors to our urban chaos. Your correspondent may not notice them, but he would certainly notice their absence as people visiting the Campbelltown Estate often remark.

Comment. Any decent-sized new estate **now** has a rule that wires be buried. Of course, this adds to the initial cost, and is one reason why new houses are so costly. It is generally agreed, I think, that such costs are worth it in the long run. In any case, it looks like underground wires will stay a while.

Assailant in Court. Peter Cocan was the name of the 20-year-old man who tried to kill Arthur Calwell. The police say he was a "loner", and he told them that he did it simply to be "set aside from other nobodies".

LETTERS IN BRIEF

No delivered milk on Sundays. Milk was still mainly home delivered, and in most areas, deliveries were seven days a week, 52 weeks a year, except for Christmas Day and Easter Friday.

Letters. Annoyed. Any person who has a large family will reject the suggestion that there should be no milk delivered on Sunday. No one has a refrigerator big enough to store enough milk for two days. In summer, we have to use our milk early in the day before it gets lumpy. If you add a second day to that, it will all be spoilt.

Some people disagreed. One person from Brisbane pointed out that **there** deliveries were not made on Sunday, and things were fine. He pitied the milkman who made deliveries every day of the year, and pointed out that in most locations, the law required the milk be on the doorstep by 7am.

One householder suggested that deliveries should be made in half-gallon bottles for large families. The Milk Board replied that a major cost for the industry was the non-return and the breakage of bottles. It argued that such losses made the cost of the bigger containers not economic.

Comment. In any case, home deliveries were on the way out. Already the rabbito, and the butcher, and the baker had been stopped by hygiene concerns. The ice-man had been frozen out by refrigerators, the fruito was giving way to the small supermarkets that were springing up. Milk was also moving to cardboard containers and Tetrapacks. It was a changing world.

Let Asians in?   **Letters.** Mr Whitlam has suggested that we should let **in a quota of educated Asians to this country**. Mr Reid has countered and said that Asians were different from each other and they are different from us. He goes on to say that the differences are so great that there is no hope of integrating them into a mass that could live together peacefully.

Another writer disagrees. If you look at Europe, you find that different racial, religious, political and other groups have fought each other for centuries. **Yet, when they come here, they can live in harmony and peace.** Surely you could expect middle-class educated Indians, Chinese and Negroes, especially if Christian, English-speaking and democratic, to do just the same. Ask yourself, why would the colour of one's skin change the behaviour of good people so much?

Beware of the dog. **Letters.** I do not want a sewing machine, Singer or otherwise. I already have a lawn mower. My carpets are fine, and I hate curtains, so blinds are what I use. But I already have a house full of blinds. My children have bikes, and we are all insured and so too is our house insured and its contents.

So, **I want all door-to-door salesmen to stay away**. Keep out, entry is forbidden, enter at your own risk, this dog bites.

Drive safely. States Transport Ministers are meeting to decide on road safety rules. They will ban passengers and drivers from **extending their elbows through open car windows. Also passengers from gutter gripping. Do you remember gutter gripping?**

NEWS ITEMS: JULY

July 1st. **Last night was Census night.** The Bureau of Statistics asked the population of the nation to declare that it was still alive and what it did and where it lived. Collectors delivered forms to every dwelling and bird cage in the nation, and will come back in a few days to collect the information. **A huge operation, made necessary by the need for planning.**

Here's a cat. Now let's find some pigeons. You will remember that the NSW Minister for Justice, Mr Maddison, said that **rents that had been pegged since about 1940 would not be raised.** This was despite the Court of Appeal saying that **increases in wages**, and also **inflation**, should be considered when fixing rents today....

On June 1st, a test case went before **the Fair Rents Board**, which was bound to accept the law. They decided, **taking into account inflation** and the like, that the rental on a test property **should be increased by 58 per cent. Did you say "58"? Yes indeed, "58". Feathers are flying in all directions....**

The knee-jerk reaction of Maddison was to say again that rents **will** not be increased, and that the Government will **legislate retrospectively to fix them at the old level. This might be harder than it sounded to him.**

June 2nd. **The French detonated a plutonium bomb** over the island of Mururoa in the central Pacific. "The big mushroom cloud has dispersed only a little, and is said to be drifting 5 degrees off its predicted course, towards South America." **Five more tests will be conducted this year. The Australian Government said it "regretted**

and deplored" the testing. On the other hand, it fully supports US testing in the same general area.

Pirate radio stations are springing up all over the world, and are a pain to governments. Small vessels, motorised or sailing, travel to areas **just outside continental limits,** and broadcast information and music onto the mainland. They are free from normal restrictions on what they can broadcast, and are often not subject to laws regarding such matters as liable. In many nations, they **make political comment that is unfavourable to the Government,** and keep a constant flow of invective on the airwaves.

Esso news. Three lions, flying in a special chartered flight from West Germany to London, **escaped from their cage.** The pilot realised this when he felt something warm and wet nuzzling his leg. He called Brussels' control tower, and was jokingly told him **to put them back in his tank.** The lions started to get nasty, and it was necessary for the pilot to fight them off with a tomahawk. The plane landed in Brussels, and the crew smashed the windscreen and escaped to safety....

The response from the control tower is very clever. Do you remember why?

Jack Brabham, famous veteran Australian racing car driver, **won the British Grand Prix.** He correctly forecast that he should not use wet-weather tyres, and won by the length of the straight. Brabham was famous for his driving in the **so-called Round-Australia Redex Trials** in the early 1950's. He was called **Gelignite Jack** for his liberal use of dynamite thrown from his car as he went through deserted country areas.

VIETNAM NEWS AND VIEWS

Holt's rebuke to Britain. Jun 8th.   Prime Minister Harold Holt supported US bombing of Hanoi, and now Haiphong, and other "strategic targets." On the other hand, **Britain has deplored the move**, saying that the situation will be inflamed and that it will lead to retaliatory bombings of the South....

In a deliberate speech today, Holt addressed Britain and regretted their attitude. He complained that Britain had no troops in Vietnam. He went on to say, ruefully, that this "is the **first time the forces of my country have been engaged in military action and have not been fighting alongside the forces of the United Kingdom**."

Bombings in Vietnam. The US bombings of North Vietnam brought forth a range of comments. Then there were others on Holt's "All the Way" promise.

Letters, Edith Bonanno. The North Vietnam air raids have done much to boost **Communist propaganda** here and overseas. Always, they report, shocking casualties have been incurred, **even when the bombing has been miles away from populated areas**.

We must remember that America is endeavouring to end this war quickly. Hitting fuel bases seems a most effective way. The fuel in question was intended to be used fighting our boys. Those who are doing the shouting here are obviously not concerned about that.

America needs our support as, after all, we have everything to lose if she fails in this struggle.

Letters, H V Crocker. In your leading article on the bombing of Hanoi and Haiphong, you infer that most Australians will support the American action.

Bearing in mind the fact that **this** country of 11 million people **failed to recruit** a mere four and a half thousand men to fight for the democratic Premier Ky **without**

resorting to conscription, it is difficult to find any reasonable grounds on which such an assumption could be based.

Letters, (Mrs) J Mason. The new Australian foreign policy announced by our Prime Minister, Mr Harold Holt, in Washington as "**all the way with LBJ**" is surely too foolish even for a nation of sheep.

Because this could lead to World War III; because if Hanoi can be bombed, so can Sydney; because already the folly of America's policy in Vietnam has become a crime against humanity – the time has come for every individual Australian to protest in writing, in speech, in personal attendance at meetings or demonstrations. What we do or do not do in the next week or so will show what kind of people we are. I hope that next year we can look back with pride and not shame at Australia in 1966.

Letters, R C Moore. The first condemnation of the bombing of oil installations in Hanoi and Haiphong came from Mr Harold Wilson of Great Britain and Mr Lester Pearson of Canada.

It is alarming to find that Britain, which had a reputation for being a champion of freedom, has reversed this policy and appears to be **on the side of the forces of Communism**, whose aim is world domination. In recent months Mr Wilson has left very little doubt as to whose side he is on.

Mr Holt, Australian Prime Minister, is to be congratulated on his support of the American action. The outcome of the war in Vietnam is of vital importance to Australia and our future lives. It is refreshing to find that our leaders are not prepared to bow to aggression and are prepared to stand up for their country.

Letters, Gina Despres, Washington, DC. The sooner Australia drops its pretence of independence and joins with the USA as the fifty-first State, the less frequently will Australians have to suffer such embarrassingly sycophantic loyalty as marks Mr Holt's present visit to Washington.

While the rest of the world, including Britain, condemns America's resumption of bombing in North Vietnam, the chief representative of the Australian people receives full military honours at the White House and publicly endorses American-Australian policy in Vietnam, because he "knows it's right."

Even Japan can assert some political and moral, if not strategic, independence, yet Australia clings to Johnson's apron-strings like a retarded child. If almost total subservience to the USA is unavoidable, the real nature of the relationship should at least be acknowledged.

Personal Comment. From the range of Letters such as these, it is becoming obvious **that public opinion on the war is becoming ossified in the short term**. By that, I mean that **most people have made up their minds**, and no matter what happens, they can find no reason to change their views. It is possible, indeed probable, that mind-changing events will **gradually** sway a few persons to veer one way or the other, but it will require a series of such events, spread over quite a few months or years, before that happens.

THAT DOG ON THAT BOX

The *SMH* printed an article by one of its journalists that talked about the town of Gundagai. Nestling quietly in the NSW country, close to the Victorian border, its population was arguing about where a new main road and bridge should be sited. It was a problem that many other communities would face over the years.

Of course, all readers will know that Gundagai was famous, not for this storm in a tea cup, but for having a dog sitting on a tucker box on the outskirts of the town. Now, let me ask you a question. "The dog sat on the tuckerbox." Everyone knows that. **But where was the tucker box?**

Silly question, you say. The answer is obvious, you might say: "nine miles from Gundagai." How do you know that? Your answer: "I remember it from school". You might be tempted to add "stupid."

The distance is five miles from Gundagai. The site of the box is actually at a camping ground for bullock teamsters in the 19th Century. The drovers'dogs were very loyal, and guarded their masters'property. One man died, and his dog sat on his tucker box for days, and would let no one near it. Hence the legend.

But let me tell you that your schoolday memory might be wrong. Ballads and songs and poems have been written about this for over a hundred years. The site where it occurred was nine miles from Gundagai, but the monument that marks it is five miles away.

So the song says five miles from Gundagai, and the poem says nine miles. In my case, I remember five as the number, but the earlier poet, Jack Mosis, used nine. He knew that was five, but he preferred the sound of nine, **because it had more music in it.**

It is still a is a bit confusing, but if you want to see the monument, try five miles first.

LIBRARIES FOR ALL?

Around 1960, most cities had a central library that they could boast about. Many large towns had inherited libraries, full of aging but popular books, from the dying local Schools of Arts. Apart from that, there were some private libraries in the suburbs and larger towns that loaned out books to members for a fee.

From 1960, the population was being gentrified in an Australian way. By this, I do **not** mean that they were heading towards the class system that still hung on in Britain. Rather, people were moving out of the working class into the middle class. Their standard of living was rising, and so too was the general level of education in the community. One sign of this was a growing demand for public libraries.

The emphasis here was on "public". What they wanted was a good collection of reading material, at some nearby locality, that was professionally run, and was financed from the public purse, and was open to everyone for free. That meant that finance had to come from somewhere, and the local Councils were the most likely source.

By 1966, perhaps a third of Councils across the nation had such libraries. Granted, they were often only at **one** central location, they might be open only three days a week, they might never open at night or in school holidays or at weekends. Still, given all that, they were there, giving good service, and making other ratepayers jealous.

They were poorly financed. Some few State Governments gave them grants on an uncertain basis. A lot of them ran from profits made by selling toffies and chocolate crackles, and from lamington drives. Gradually, Councils bit the bullet, and used ratepayers' money to pay capital costs and wages. Local Council Public libraries were on their way.

But it was over many dead bodies. The biggest cause of resistance was straight from the hip pocket. There were **three versions of this**. **The first** was from rate payers who said that roads and parks should get first priority on Council spending. **The second** came from a group who said that they would never use a library. Why should they pay for one?

The third said that that there were many people who paid no rates. Why should they get to use a library free while others paid for them?

So, the controversies dragged on, but little by little, Council by Council, libraries were adopted, and have **now** been accepted by all local authorities.

Here are a few **other** thoughts on the matter, back in 1966.

Letters, J Masters. I have recently lived in French's Forest where there is a large High school with another one proposed for nearby Killarney. There is no easily accessible **public library with trained librarians** in attendance here. Some schools have good libraries, of course, but they are not available during the nearly three months of school holiday yearly. In the last long summer vacation I visited a children's library at Forestville which I believe is privately run, but it was closed for the entire school holiday.

There is tremendous interest in this country in education. But whatever is the use of new school buildings and new schemes if the whole process of educative reading is cut the moment school is out? Where does the remedy lie?

Letters, J Sedgwick, Children's Library Movement. I have been actively engaged in running the Narrabeen Children's Library for 13 years with a small group of similarly interested women. It operates throughout the year except for a period of two weeks at Christmas time when it has to close because of shortage of helpers.

The facilities for the children are in existence at the moment, and if there were more people interested enough to volunteer their help, existing libraries could be greatly expanded. **The need is not money but more helpers.**

Comment. These Letters (and others) cover only problems with **childrens' books**. But **what about the general public? Can adults use libraries too?**

Letters, Dot Martin, Queensland country. Our children are being spoiled. They get better houses, and better education, and better food, and better health care than the generation that gave birth to them. Good luck to them, I say. But sometimes it goes too far.

I have in mind the large volume of letters to your paper about libraries. They dwell mainly on childrens' libraries. I put it to you that a generation of parents need public libraries much more than the kid's do, because they did not get the same education level. And school libraries, no matter how small, do cater for the young ones. So they are getting their fair share of books and libraries.

But take persons like myself. I had a poor education, but would like to fix that. One way to do that is to get books from libraries, and study them. But I have no library within *Cooee*. There are a few that are in range, but adults can't use them. There are a few in schools. But again, I can't use them.

Am I to go to my grave in my current ignorant condition?

There was another argument. There was a split developing within the body of library-lovers. **One faction** wanted general reading books, like fiction and romances and adventure.

A second faction wanted more academic works, and reference and educative books. Clearly there would not be enough money for both, it was said, so a choice would have to be made. There was no unanimity apparent.

Finally, back to the hip pocket.

Letters, E Hunt. As a Kogarah ratepayer I support Mr M Forbes, our deputy town clerk, who asked whether a library was a fair burden for a council to bear.

We have some 48,000 residents in this municipality, and only 14,000 are ratepayers. Let us wait until some plan is evolved to allow the other 34,000 people to share the cost before consideration is given to a library.

Kogarah ratepayers require their representatives to confine their activities to matters strictly municipal and not to meddle with anything else. We owe a king's ransom as it is!

Comment. Some friends of mine do regular surveys of the attitude of rate payers to Council expenditures. They assure me that the same three resistant attitudes persist today over fifty years later. Granted they are now held by a small minority, but they argue that if ever Councils got into serious financial difficulties, then the clock would be turned back, and **the libraries would be the first to go**. Perhaps they are right. Then again, maybe they are wrong. **I hope we never find out.**

A JAUNDICED MOMENT: TWO MORALS

I enclose a Letter, and add two morals. **First, the Letter.**

Mr L Aarons, Secretary of the Communist Party of Australia, sought to correct the *SMH* report of a meeting held by the Maritime Branch recently.

Firstly, he said, you reported that less than half the expected 100 attended. **That report was wrong.** 107 attended.

Secondly, the reports said that there had been a decline in membership, and that Branch amalgamations have thus occurred. **That report is wrong.** The opposite is the case. The amalgamations occcurred because growth in membership permitted more democratic discussion and demanded efficiencies.

Thirdly, he goes on, you reported that I warned of stern battles with shipowners and the Federal Government. You said that I talked of conscripting seamen to take supplies to Vietnam. **These reports were wrong.**

Mr Aarons said that his remarks dealt with **changes in our social forces. Not with any of the other matters you accused me of.**

Now the first moral. Don't believe everything you read in the newspaper.

Of course, you know already not to do this. It is just that at the moment, the newspapers and the air waves are so full of American and Governmental pro-war propaganda, and anti-Red propaganda, that I am getting jaundiced.

Take the Letter above. **You would have to believe what it says.** After all, **the *SMH* is always quick to refute any charges that its reports are not accurate**, but it does not do so on this occasion. You then hopefully accept that the report of the meeting was wrong and deliberately so.

Before I get accused of being a Red-sympathiser, let me say you could substitute "Girl Guides" for "Reds" and my conclusion would be the same. That is, that the paper was so intent on its mission of prosecuting the Reds that it lost track of the facts.

The second moral is that in war, the enemy's actions and motives are always subjected to distortion. As has been said so often, **there is no truth in war.**

LETTERS IN BRIEF

Australian royalty? **Letters.** The *SMH* described **Mr and Mrs Holt** as **"Australia's first couple."** A Mr Daintree objected. He said that the term could only apply to the Queen and Prince Phillip. Or, if you stretched the point, it could apply to the Governor General couple. But to the Holts, no way. He also regretted the **perceived implication that royalty could be replaced by commoners**.

Doffing the lid. **Letters.** Schoolboys leaving a Sydney private school were observed **raising their hats to stopping motorists** at pedestrian crossings. It was pointed out that this was not a sign of the good values taught **at the school**, but rather a sign of the good manners and values taught **at home**. These homes were worthy of the honour and glory bestowed on the boys.

Belt up and live. **Letters.** Two country doctors wrote a Letter that pointed out that lives had been saved by wearing seat belts, and the truly gruesome consequences of not wearing them. They pointed out that in their region less than 20 per cent of drivers used belts.

They advocated forcibly that all drivers **should be compelled to wear belts at all times.** They stressed that it **was not good enough** to make it compulsory only for **new vehicles**. This is pretty radical thinking, and certain to meet a lot of resistance.

A different type of Letter spoke of a different aspect of the matter.

Letters, D I Banks. Two years ago I bought a new car and had safety belts fitted to the two front seats.

It takes only a few seconds only to slip into and fasten mine. When carrying a passenger, I always invite him or her to do the same. In this two years, I would say that only one passenger in 10 has made the first move, or acquiesced willingly, to fasten themselves in. The other nine have either laughed self-consciously or made some deprecating remark and declined. When I say, "Well, suit yourself, that's the suicide seat, anyway!" 90 per cent of them sheepishly don the belt and the remainder continue to trust to their luck.

It is not sufficient merely to campaign for installation of seat belts, but also the wearing of them.

Comment. You might remember that not long after this, a number of road authorities of various States used my introductory heading, "Belt up and Live", as the catch-cry for their advertising.

Vast swindle by PMG. Many people were unhappy with the performance of the phone system. They claimed the PMG was **taking money but delivering phone services that were not adequate**. They cited crossed lines, humming roars in the lines, and incorrect engaged signals. They were finding that wrong numbers were common, that persistent crackling on the line made communication not possible, that the message was so weak that the other person could not be heard. Public phones had the additional problem that half of them were out of action.

A farmer concludes with a little vitriol. "The loss of work-time would exceed that due to alcoholism, TV, football post-mortems, morning tea, grandmothers' funerals, and putting on lip-stick.

Our female models. **Letters.** What pictures of dignity, grace and beauty are presented to us by the groups of Asian students and others, as shown in the Press and on TV from time to time.

They are in marked contrast to the pictures of our own "models of fashion." The latter shock me and fill me with a sense of distaste and dismay.

Clothing is skimpy, ugly, and ill-cut; shoes barbaric; hair unkempt and often dirty-looking; complexions piled over with all sorts of foreign matter, even the eyes; postures most inelegant with no respect for modesty. Whatever evil influence induces our beautiful women to submit to such despoilation.

Not talking to any driver. **Letters**. We have all seen the sign on buses saying "*Do not talk to the driver while the bus is in motion*". I suggest that it should be put in all private cars and trucks also. You might say that it takes a lot of fun out of having a sociable trip, and prevents the driver from joining in to conversations.

But you need to weigh this up against having smashes and being killed and maimed. If you think about it, **it's better to have a silent driver than a dead one**.

AUGUST NEWS ITEMS

Australia is about to get its first **shipping container port,** at Sydney. It will have a frontage of 2,666 feet to the harbour, and a depth of 400 feet. It will be connected to the rail system.

An unofficial war crimes tribunal, in London, will "try" President Johnson on charges that America's conduct of the Vietnam war **involves crimes against humanity.** Specifically, the charges include the use of "chemicals, gas, and saturation bombing of an entire area with jelly-gasoline and phosphorus." Also with the widespread use of napalm on villages and forests....

The tribunal will include 14 distinguished people, and be **headed by philosopher Bertrand Russel.** It will sit for 12 weeks, and be reported in full in papers and film. It will bring in 200 North Vietnamese victims to give evidence....

This is clearly an anti-war stunt, calculated to gain publicity. Its verdict will have no consequences at all, but the day-to-day proceedings should provide many headlines.

Well-known **Australia jockey Scobie Beasly** some years ago went to England for fame and fortune. On August 7th he **won his 2,000[th] race in England.**

In New Guinea, a dispute over a game of cards on a plantation led **to the axe-murder of one native.** The dead man's tribesmen then **axe-murdered two other men in their sleep in retaliation.**

Some very good news on the South East Asia front. **Indonesia and Malaysia officially ended their on-again-off-again hostilities on August 12th.**

The world premiere of **the film *"They're a Weird Mob"* opened in Sydney.** The author, John O'Grady, as well as the leads, Walter Chiari and Clare Dunn, were on hand.

17 Australian soldiers were killed, and 26 wounded in a battle with the Viet Cong in South Vietnam today. **Eleven of the dead, and 13 of the wounded were National Servicemen....**

A young blond girl from Brisbane **received a marriage proposal** from one of the young soldiers **this morning. She learned in the afternoon that he had been killed.**

A clergyman in New York believes **the Beatles music is profane and blasphemous.** This Saturday night, he will combat the Beatles when they perform in the 14,400 seat Civic Auditorium. **He has announced that he will conduct a rival hymn-singing in direct challenge** to the Liverpool **quartet in a near-by hall.** He has an advantage. He is offering free entry....

The clergyman was not successful. **His church attracted only a handful of people.** The Beatles had a full house, and the next day had to escape in an armoured van when 45,000 fans mobbed them at the Dodgers Baseball Stadium. Apparently, **profanity and blasphemy sell really well.**

Peter Cocan, the attempted assailant of Arthur Calwell, was found guilty of attempted murder, and **sentenced to life imprisonment**. The Court found that was he was mentally disordered to some extent, but fit to plead....

He said that "I am deeply sorry about what has happened. There is **not the slightest personal malice against Mr Calwell.** I just felt it was inevitable, I am deeply sorry. That's all". Calwell comforted Cocan's mother. Observers could not offer any real explanation for Cocan's behaviour.

The average cost of a new home in Sydney will be $8,600 in 1966.

VIETNAM NEWS AND VIEWS

The US Ambassador at the time, Ed Clark, was not notable for his tact. He was strongly of the opinion that America had never done any wrong, and that it never could. So, when he entertained a luncheon in Canberra with his pro-US wisdom from WWII, no one was really surprised. But some people were angry. He said that the British do not have a sufficiently long memory to remember that the US "pulled their chessnuts out of the fire 25 years ago." By this, he meant that America had entered the war (late), and then had contributed arms and men that helped lead to an Allied victory.

Letters, R H Thouless. Our memories must be defective since we have no memory of the USA fighting by our side against the Nazi aggression in Poland in 1939. Poland was a long way from America, and the Americans may well have thought that aggression in Poland was not their business.

So defective are our memories that we suppose that when France fell in 1940, Great Britain and the Commonwealth were left to fight alone against Germany until a year later Russia entered the fight and six months after that the United States was led to declare war by the Pearl Harbour incident.

The British people would urge their Government to give military support to the USA in Vietnam if they thought that was a right course of action. They would **not** do so because they remembered that the United States gave them late military support in their own much greater danger.

Letters, Brian E Heawood. In the same issue, the US Ambassador, Mr Edward Clark, is reported as saying, clearly in reference to the British people, "We pulled their chestnuts out of the fire 25 years ago." This, said in a country which still regards itself as predominantly

British, seems to be in questionable taste. No doubt Mr Clark is peeved with Mr Wilson for refusing to go "all the way with LBJ," but this hardly excuses his implication that the British are showing ingratitude to his own country for winning "their" war for them.

If top-level courtesies between friends can be degraded to these levels, it is hardly surprising that US and Australian Government leaders should glory in the avowed "dirtiness" of the war against the Communist enemies, or that they should appear to be less sincerely in earnest to achieve a peaceful settlement than other responsible world leaders.

Letters, P J Milton. In World War I, Britain and her Empire lost thousands of men fighting aggression before the United Sates came in at the end (three years after it started).

Likewise in World War II – two years after it had begun – the United States entered – not freely, but only because she was attacked by Japan. But for Pearl Harbour it is doubtful whether she would have entered at all. She would have been content to let the British Empire fight it out by herself and certainly wouldn't have worried if Britain's "chestnuts" were burnt.

Let's be fair. If the struggle in Vietnam continues for three years, and Britain hasn't entered then, Mr Clark can shout with some justification.

Comment. These Letters show that the bragging of **some** Americans that "they won the war", and their disparaging remarks about the Allies' contributions, were still well remembered in Australia.

Of course, Clark's real aim was to change political opinion in Britain. At the moment, Britain was snarling at America for its intervention in Vietnam, and it (Britain) was sending no men or materials into the fray. Clark was saying that, since America had (reluctantly and profitably) saved Britain in WWII, Britain should pitch in and help in Vietnam. That is one way of thinking. **But there are other ways.**

SPREAD ALL OVER THE PLACE

Here we have the topic of the month. It would be easy to say it was the real beginning of the war between butter and margarine. But that would very much over-simplify.

The debate was started by a long Letter from a Professor at the University of NSW. He said that there was a strong association between the level of cholesterol and coronary heart disease. He went on to argue that **margarine should be substituted for butter**. Then followed a long reply, amid a heap of statistics, that said that the preference for margarine was not justified.

After that, **Letters flowed in to the *SMH***. They appeared under headings like *Saturated Fats*, *Diet's Effect on Health*, *Butter versus Margarine*, *Courageous Stand*, *High Pressure Stand*, and *Why All the Fuss?* Many of them were so full of statistics as to be meaningless. There were stats for NZ, Britain, Europe, America, India, and of course Australia. There were production stats, stats on the incidence of diseases, average age of death, butter consumption, margarine consumption, saturated versus unsaturated consumption, cancer-causing agents, and what have you. I'm sure there would have been the *Average Age at Birth* included there somewhere if I had looked.

So the battle raged. The vital question was whether it was butter or margarine that you should spread on your sandwiches and use in your cooking. The people who got the most space in the Letters column were entities like Marrickville Holdings, (for margarine), the Professor mentioned above (for margarine), Dorrigo Dairy Company (for butter), and the Australian Jersey Herd Society (for butter). They fought their pitched battles of opinions and out-of-date selective statistics for a full month.

Meanwhile, a few ordinary consumers got a small word in.

Letters, H Vains. In all the hullabaloo about margarine quotas, the debate seems to be losing perspective.

Evidence suggests that table margarine has been freely available for some time throughout Australia. Therefore, if margarine quotas were removed, how could this in itself lead to an immediate and unprecedented increase in demand, which is what the dairying industry appears to fear most?

Some people will always prefer butter to margarine and vice versa. Some people need butter – particularly children – others do not. Why so much concern?

Letters, Eileen Ridley. If adequate supplies of margarine are prevented from reaching the public, it may be no tragedy for the well-to-do, but would definitely be so for poorer people, especially pensioners. Many such folk cannot afford butter at all and for them, margarine forms a welcome and healthy substitute. To restrict its production may mean that many of these unfortunate ones may have to go without altogether. This appears to be a most callous move, and a sad reflection upon our "free" country, especially at a time when Governments all over the world are calling for more production.

Comment. You might notice that in the above report I was a bit offhand. That was because I have seen over the years so many marketing campaigns fought through the columns of the Press with claim and counter-claim flowing back and forth, often for years. This is especially true, I think, in matters relating to food and the like. To take an extreme case, for years we were told that unscraped blackened toast would give us cancer.

In this case, butter versus margarine, I am sure that, 50 years later, the matter has not been settled to the satisfaction of all. I am also sure that **it never will be** while large vested interests are still fighting for the same market. Really, humans being humans, it is not about the health effects of the products at all, but rather about whether someone's market share is 50.3 or perhaps 50.4 per cent this month.

THE PILL BRIEFLY

The contraceptive Pill was under siege from conservative elements, some of whom feared that women would lose their virtue to temptation. Others, particularly the Catholic Church, believed that its use was to deny the **main purpose of sexual intercourse, which was supposedly to propagate**. In any case, many elements in society were waging a campaign against its use.

From the pulpit it was thundered that the sin involved was mortal. From some women's magazines, there were stories of deformities to both mother and future children if it was used. From moralists came warnings that society would crumble when women were released from the bondage that fortunately had kept them in place. Australia's birth-rate too would tumble, and the evil Asians were just waiting for such a chance to pounce.

Despite all this, the Pill, now in its third year of widespread usage in Australia, was gradually getting more women to swallow it. **Its** market share continued to climb.

INEBRIATES ACT

I bring to your attention, without further comment, the following touching Letter.

Letters, (Mrs) Marjorie F Cole. In deep distress of mind, I should like to draw your readers' attention to the Inebriates Act of 1912. I have close contact with a near relative suffering from one of the worst diseases – alcoholism. He has, over the years, spent months in psychiatric hospitals and he is at present in one of these. It is the considered opinion of the medical profession that he is in need of 12 months in Kenmore or Morisset hospital for treatment, yet his loving relatives **must bring a charge against him, must appear in court and give evidence against him, forcing him to appear also.**

These alcoholics are ill in mind, body and soul. Their relatives spend much time, effort and deep thought in how best to help them, yet under the rigours of an archaic law, they are forced to treat them as some sort of criminal, forcing them to appear in a court of law. We are sometimes grateful that other diseases are not so barbarously dealt with. May God lighten our darkness!

DOGS IN FOCUS

I know most of you have been fretting about how dogs are doing in 1966. The latest news is just in, and I give it to you in its natural, unedited state. Straight from the horse's mouth.

Letters, D R Macdonald. A good section of the community is seething over the increase from 25 cents to $2 in the cost of a dog licence. The exponents of this increase say it is a move to rid communities of stray and unnecessary dogs that are not properly tended. I say that probably 90 per cent of dogs are well looked after.

There will always be a few unwanted and roaming dogs, but surely owners have a big enough problem to feed their dogs considering the rather exorbitant price of meat.

This grab is a rapier-thrust at the family pet, while the usefulness and necessity of the dog in the pastoral industry does not seem to have been considered at all.

Letters, K A Smith. May I assure Mr MacDonald that a larger, thoughtful section of the community **approves the increased dog licence fee** and applauds the politically courageous Askin Government's effort to clean up another shameful facet of NSW living – indiscriminate breeding of dogs, the disgraceful number of strays, unrestricted, uncontrolled and unregistered ownership, and the shocking hygienic habits of a community in which dogs are allowed, and encouraged by some owners, to foul footpaths and grass plots.

Letters, (Mrs) J Curson. In two months the dog registration fee rises to $2 – quite an appreciable jump. I would ask all owners of dogs during the next two months to give the matter of their dogs' future careful and serious thought.

If they find that they will be unable to keep the dogs at the increased rate, please do not wait until that "Doggy Doomsday" and then secretly and shamefully dump them somewhere. Surely in the two coming months they could save enough to pay for **their dogs' painless destruction** by a qualified veterinarian. If their dog has meant anything at all to them, then pay him the tribute of a dignified death.

If their dog is a family "mutt," think what his loss is going to mean to his playmates. In the forthcoming two months, encourage them to put in a little each week toward his retention.

Surely with three choices – (1) pay for him yourself (even at the cost of a few cigarettes), (2) have him painlessly destroyed, or (3) bring the kids into it – there should be no need for any more stray dogs to join the unfortunate thousands that already roam our streets through our fault, and ours only.

LETTERS IN BRIEF

Crime and Migrants. **Letters.** It had been said a number of times recently that migrants committed disproportionally more crimes. A number of Commissions over the last decade have looked at this and have reported that quite the reverse is true. This is especially so for serious crimes.

Road toll. Letters. Here is a new idea. In New Zealand, the police are equipped with radar speed detectors. One officer sits in the stationary car and measures the speed of an oncoming vehicle. They either flag it down, or pass on the number to another police car further along the road.

This method would appear to be safer than used in Australian States. For example, chasing a sports car at 100 miles per hour until it crashes.

Comment. It's hard to see Australian motorists standing for that type of interference. **We will never see it in Australia.**

Help for Vietnamese. **Letters, Sheila Rowley, Vietnam Relief Fund.** You were kind enough to publish a letter on our behalf appealing for contributions to a fund for the civilian victims of the war in South Vietnam. Contributions already amount to $2,233 – a generous response in nine days. We shall keep the fund open until September 30.

As the expenses of the fund have been covered by donations for that purpose from inside the University of New South

Wales, every cent donated by the public will go to the Kontum Mission for distribution to the people Bishop Seitz described.

Tolerance towards transistors. *Letters.* A reader is surprised by the tolerance shown to the owners of transistors that are played on public transport. He is not inclined to risk an ugly scene, and finds that most other people glance sidelong at each other, and grin and bear it. Some legal limits should be placed on the volumes that will be allowed, and they should be backed up with notices displaying the fines payable if the limits are exceeded.

The Beatles in the US. **The Beatles were performing in the USA to big crowds.** But outside the performances, they have sometimes met with crowds who accosted them because of their supposed blasphemy. Occasionally the scenes got a bit out of hand, and minor scuffles occurred.

One girl, reported in the London Press, said "if the Yanks do anything to the Beatles, it will be the start of World War III."

A little mystery. This *Letter* appeared without any reference. I have been not able to trace its genesis. But it is too intriguing to leave out. It appeared under the heading of "The Case Against Ned Kelly."

Letters, Sidney J Baker. Now that the white-washers (including the Jerilderie hillbillies) have moved in to defend the moronic Ned Kelly, I hope you will excuse me if I raise a small point.

It is this: Apart from a few scrappy Press and TV reports, my case against Ned Kelly and his gang of homosexuals has not been examined by the public. Ergo, Douglas Stewart et al have only the flimsiest ideas of what they are dealing with.

As for being a character assassin, I can't help asking this simple question: How on earth is it possible to assassinate the character of a murderer, a thief, a liar and a lout?

***Charges made by undertakers.* Letters.**   Most of us know little of undertakers' charges until the "unwelcome visitor" takes away one of our relatives.

A charge of $300 to $400 is not unusual for an ordinary funeral. To make sure of being paid, some undertakers demand a deposit before acting at all, and then add interest to the cost, deductible if the account is paid within a month.

While not exactly moaning, may I enter a stiff protest at such a grave overcharge.

Comment.   The writer worked hard to get in the puns on the last line. That aside, the cost of funerals was a recurring theme in 1966. Since then, it is my impression that the cost of a basic funeral has remained about the same (relative to inflation), though the current trend towards elaborate ceremonies with full theatrical effects and audience participation can increase the costs greatly.

***Turning the tables.* Sydney is experiencing a spate of bank robberies this year**. Since the year started, **38 robberies have been attempted**. Most have been armed hold-ups, though 11 have been through opening safes. Today, the largest heist in Australia's history was successful when a Bank of NSW branch in the city **was relieved of $103,000 from a safe**.

SEPTEMBER NEWS ITEMS

The Premier of NSW is troubled by **the cost of building roads**. His State already has one toll road, to the Hawkesbury, but he says that more will be needed. "**Toll roads are widely built in USA and Europe**. It is not just NSW that will need to charge for usage of long-distance highways. **Every State in the Commonwealth will need to build them, and soon**".

September 6th. **The South African Prime Minister, Hendrik Werwoerd, was stabbed to death in Parliament** today by a white assailant....

An earlier attempt was made on Werwoerd's life in 1960 when a white man fired two shots into his head at an international Trade Fair in Johannesburg. Worwoerd was seen as "**the epitome of South Africa's apartheid policy.**"

At next year's monster **"Expo 67" in Montreal in Canada**, the Australian contingent to perform has been nominated. **Do you remember them?** Their names include The Seekers, Rolf Harris, and teenage idol Normie Rowe. Robert Helpmann will be there, with Bobby Limb and Kathy Lloyd. A former Tivoli star, Frank Donellan, will give a boomerang-throwing exhibition.

The British Commonwealth is in disarray. This has become obvious at a week-long meeting of the heads of all the Commonwealth countries in London this week. **The focal point is Rhodesia** where the Prime Minister, Ian Smith, has imposed laws to maintain white supremacy. Britain and the Commonwealth objected to this, and Smith is now making **serious threats to leave the Commonwealth**. He is not attending the current meeting….

The African nations are talking (sometimes wildly) about Britain using force on Rhodesia, and overthrowing Smith, and imposing black rule. Britain wants to impose sanctions and then persuasion on Smith. Australia wants to talk about Vietnam, hoping the Brits will join in there. This is a mess that will need clever handling, **otherwise the Commonwealth could have more than Rhodesia on the move.**

Baccarat is illegal, but there are well-known schools in all capital cities. A *SMH* reporter went into one of these and told his story of the hundreds of players winning and losing money. He noted that if you lost, **on exit you were given one dollar for your fare home, and one all-day sucke**r.

What do **Test cricket Captains** do after they retire from the game? It's hard to speak for all of them, but one of them, **Lindsay Hassett, popped up pulling the marbles from the barrel for the Nasho quarterly lottery**.

Dogmen are doomed. The NSW Labour Council decided that the **men who ride on the hooks of cranes** should no longer be allowed to do that, due to safety concerns. This follows the death of two of them recently….

The spectacle of the dogman, balancing in the crane hook or on timber being hoisted, will be denied to pedestrians in future. Dogmen are disappointed because **they were previously paid danger money for their rides**.

Victorian policeman, Reg Henderson, has **a photographic memory. He has arrested more than 300 people** after recognising them in the streets.

VIETNAM NEWS AND VIEWS.

Letters, Paul S Seitz, Bishop of Kontum, South Vietnam. To escape the terrors of war, 400,000 people have fled from their homes. Many have sought shelter in Catholic missions in my diocese of Kontum. The condition of these refugees is pitiful and desperate in the extreme. They need food, clothing, shelter and – most of all – medical attention. Three out of four babies are dying, and more than six out of ten children are starving, or sick with malaria and dysentery.

The only wish of these innocent people is to live their lives in peace like normal families the world over. The politics of the Great Powers are beyond their understanding. They are simple souls, and in their tragedy they have turned to us, as Christ's missionaries. Can we make their sick babies well? Can we cure their diseases? Have we any food?

Comment. His letter ended with an appeal for funds for relief.

I should mention at this stage that the war is getting worse **for the villagers**. By this, I mean that reports say US bombing is increasing in severity. What happens is that the active Viet Cong escape from the US (and Australian) troops, and enter villages. The villagers hide them, and so the US Air Force drops napalm bombs on the villages.

This has been going on for months. It is now reportedly happening more widely. On top of this, the bombs, when dropped on jungle, defoliate the vegetation, and make the Viet Cong visible and easy to attack. This is a new device, and is adding to the deaths of the local population.

RHODESIA NOW A PROBLEM

The Rhodesian situation had been festering for a year. Prime Minister Smith, firmly in power, was determined that control by the whites should not be curtailed, and had recently announced that he would withdraw from the Commonwealth because this body was pressuring him to allow changes. The Brits, as head of the Commonwealth, said that they would not accept his resignation. No one really understood what that meant. Would such a silly situation spread to other countries? Would the old British Empire, once so strong, now disintegrate as one nation after another went its own way? Should the United Nations be called in to do something? But, if so, what could it do?

No one had any idea. Or more accurately, everyone had an idea, but no two people had the same idea. Hence the mess at the conference in London that was described above.

Passions in Australia were stirred and Letters were written. Here is a sample of one line of opinion.

Letters, (Rev) B J Dooley. You are wrong when you say recently that **"no Australian will accept for a moment** that **our soldiers should be used in Rhodesia."**

I do accept it, and so do many Australians. The only way to minimise – and probably entirely prevent – bloodshed is to confront the illegal tyranny which calls itself the "Government" of Rhodesia with overwhelming force from the whole British Commonwealth of Nations.

Treason against the Crown is a worse crime than murder, and to allow a privileged white minority to get away with it will be to destroy our multi-racial commonwealth of nations, which in the long run may well be worth more to Australia than even an all-white American alliance.

If it is right to send Australian soldiers to Vietnam, it would be much more so to send them to Rhodesia. World peace requires justice for all races, therefore the restoration of lawful government in Rhodesia matters tremendously to Australia.

Were there a call for volunteers to fight **against** the Smith rebel regime, you would be very surprised at the response

Letters, John M Turner. I read with astonishment and dismay the remarks of the Rev B Dooley. In his intemperate letter, he advocated the use of force by British and Commonwealth troops to overthrow the present regime in Rhodesia, and suggested that Australian volunteers participate in military actions against their own blood brothers and kinsmen.

Mr Dooley described the Smith Government "as an illegal tyranny," and accused it of treason against the Crown.

Illegal in an accepted sense it may be, tyrannous it is not, as any fair-minded visitor to Rhodesia will testify, including the Bantu tribal chiefs themselves.

Rhodesia continues to fly the Union Jack at every masthead (the only country in Africa to do so), portraits of her Majesty remain in every building, and the majority of Rhodesians continue unswerving in their allegiance to the Queen.

They have rebelled against a mean, spiteful, vindictive, British Socialist Prime Minister, whose policy would precipitate a bloodbath of murder anarchy and chaos; the inevitability of which has been evidenced in Congo, Tanzania, Ghana and Nigeria.

Advocacy of violence by a clergyman appals me, and incitement of Australians to volunteer for service against Rhodesia is even worse.

If pressure from people like Mr Dooley prevailed, I in my turn can assure him that I know many Australians, including myself, who will serve with, and **for,** the Rhodesians and Mr Smith.

Letters, S Thompson, Gladesville. What wishful thinking prompts the Rev B Dooley to believe that Australians would fight against their own kith and kin in Rhodesia because of their declaration of independence? **I would think there would be more volunteers to assist Ian Smith's cause than we would get to fight in Vietnam!**

Here at least we have a courageous leader recognising the pressure of Communist influence in Africa who won't be intimidated. The return to barbarism that has occurred in neighbouring African States is a warning that if the benefits of Western influence are to endure in this unhappy continent, men like Ian Smith and his loyal Rhodesians need support, not condemnation.

Comment. Despite numerous conferences with Britain and lots of other Commonwealth countries, Smith maintained his racist stance, against growing opposition, until he lost the position of Prime Minister in 1987 to the black Robert Mugabe. In the meantime, many lives were lost as battles and riots occurred in pursuit of **equality and self rule for the blacks**. But, **a reminder**, this was more or less what was happening over half of Africa from the southernmost tip of South Africa to the shores of Tripoli.

IRRITATIONS AT THE MOVIES

As if wars in Vietnam and aggro in Rhodesia are not enough to bear, there is another plague tearing society apart.

Many writers were complaining about the distractions and annoyances at movie theatres. On top of the list was going into a city theatre after one session had finished, and finding that it was strewn with rubbish, ranging from empty drink bottles, to half-eaten ice cream cones, to cigarette butts and boxes.

"The usherette showed the way with a torch, and led us to our four booked seats. Very nice these were too, situated with a good full view of the screen. The only trouble was that monkeys had been there the previous session, and the seats and floor were fully occupied with peanut shells."

A second problem was the constant talkers during the screenings. One prominent journalist took the cudgel to these miscreants, and says that she has not once attended a film this year without this annoyance. No amount of cajoling can get the yappers to stop for long, but apparently news of their operations, and slimming treatments, and neighbours' excesses is too valuable to wait till the end of the session.

"Perhaps the bad manners could be partially **explained** because women have got used to talking during TV, but it **can't be excused**."

Letters, George Williams. Many cheers for Tess Van Sommers and her protest concerning ignorant yappers at the cinema.

I am a retired man, and a sufferer from a heart complaint. Whenever I attend a morning session at the cinema I am invariably irritated beyond endurance and have to move one or more times to escape the incessant "yap" of middle-aged females. As aggravation sometimes outweighs entertainment, I react by staying away from the cinema for weeks. Annoyance is best avoided by those whose hearts are not healthy.

May I also ask how much longer we must endure *God Save the Queen* before a few dozen patrons may watch a mid-morning film? What pompous stupidity it is to expect the cardiacs, the cripples, the obese, the arthritic, the aged, and the plain weary, to struggle to their feet for this meaningless and widely resented incongruity! Why don't we have to sing grace, too? Some time ago I determined not to stand up any more, and I do not. It is not that I lack patriotism; it is just that I have some commonsense and some moral courage.

Let us hope that managements will drop *God Save the Queen* at minor matinees and think more in terms of "God help the audience" and protect them against pests. If they don't, a few more patrons will indubitably prefer to stay away.

Mr Williams was touching on an increasingly sore point when he spoke about standing for *God Save the Queen*. Audiences were starting to question this relic from the days of the Empire, with its pink maps and photos of the British monarch on most public walls. They were asking why should they have to overtly display their unquestioned loyalty at each and every public occasion.

Mostly, they were not as yet deliberately republican. They still supported the Royals, they liked their various links to Britain, and they still flocked in their millions to watch the Queen whenever she visited. It was just that a different spirit was strong throughout the land, one that said we want none of the relics of the old imperial world that kept us repressed in pre-war years. **No one was prepared to dip their lid anymore.**

Other writers added their bit.

Letters, C Cody. I am with George Williams all the way in his protest about the playing of "God Save the Queen".

It is nothing but sheer annoyance at an entertainment. They don't have it in England. I am not as brave as Mr

Williams, though. My method is to get up slowly and sit down quickly and early.

Still, at least one writer thought it was a good thing. It would be interesting to hear the reasons why.

Letters, D W Watts. If a man with a weak heart can get himself to the cinema, he can presumably stand, and, unless he is sitting on the front row, there is the back of a seat on which he can lean.

Infirmity and personal prejudice may perhaps be good excuses for not standing during the playing of the National Anthem, but they do not warrant its ability. I can assure C Cody that it is still played in England and that Englishmen still stand.

EAGLES

Australia was apparently gun happy. Throughout the country regions, the Papers were full of shooting parties riding into the bush at the weekends and blasting away at anything that moved. That is, after they had demolished all the road signs on the way to their shack.

This was in an era when gun laws were not severe and when they were virtually ignored by anyone outside of the capital cities. Of course, there were legal shooting seasons, for ducks, and ferrals, and for miscreants like wild boar, and occasionally even for roos. But there was **some** semblance of control over these, so the most extreme adventures were reserved for the week-end wild men and women.

Complaints, and pleas for better behaviours, made their way regularly to the papers. But this first Letter captured the spirit of the times. The second is for those of you who are wondering if your family eagle can become a menace when you are not at home keeping an eye on it.

Letters, J Morrison. Some months ago, walking in the Blue Mountains near Katoomba, I stopped to admire a pair of eagles circling effortlessly in the blue of the sky.

Recently in the same area, I again saw what was probably one of the same two eagles, dead. It had been shot and the proud "sportsman" had spread-eagled it along a paddock fence as a sort of scarecrow. It was a magnificent brown eagle with a 6-foot wingspan.

Nearby were the rotting old carcasses of a steer and a sheep. It is a fair guess that this eagle was shot while feeding off them.

What makes people shoot a rare and magnificent bird like an eagle? **There is still no evidence that eagles kill or even attack lambs**, although they may feed off dead stock (if anyone knows to the contrary I shall be interested to hear it).

Why is the eagle not protected by law as in other countries? Is it to become almost shot out of existence like the North American condor or (to come nearer home) to become what our koala has become, and the kangaroo is fast becoming, a "tourist curiosity"? Is sheer public indifference again letting trigger-happy maniacs have the final say in denuding our wilderness areas of any remaining wildlife?

Letters, S Fuller. Mr Morrison said: "There is still no evidence that eagles kill or even attack lambs," and he invited anyone who knows anything contrary to advise him of it.

Many years ago when employed on a sheep property adjoining the Warrumbungle Ranges in Western New South Wales (a great nesting-place for eagles) I witnessed the following incident. A large wedge-tail eagle, which had been circling above a mob of ewes and lambs for some time, suddenly swooped down and deliberately cut off a six-months-old lamb from the mob, driving it away, and at the same time flew over it, repeatedly beating it to the ground with its wings. The lamb was on the point of exhaustion when I intervened and drove the eagle off. I had never seen such a thing, but I am convinced that eagles do attack and kill lambs.

On another occasion, I rode upon a ewe recently killed, and surrounded by half a dozen dead lambs, which she had evidently been trying to protect. All the evidence pointed to this being the work of eagles, and not crows.

While admiring the mobility of these birds of prey (I have counted 62 in the air at one time, and over 20 on one carcass), I know them to be ruthless destroyers of lambs and, in some cases, grown sheep.

Comment. A handful of people, all from the outback, wrote in and left no doubt that eagles attacked lambs and sheep. Some said that the current drought conditions have killed all the rabbits, and so only the crows and eagles survived. But scarcity of small prey left the eagles hungry, and they were currently attacking sheep commonly. They nearly all said that the first step in the attack was to pick the eyes out of the victim. But one added that when he sought to protect a particular sheep by putting a cloth round its eyes, when he came back the skull and brain were found to be ripped off.

I conclude that eagles do in fact attack sheep. The Secretary of the Royal Ornithologists' Union admits that, but points out that the deaths caused by eagles are still few in number, and that eagles do have other virtues. He adds "Unfortunately, too many gun shops and magazines foster this slaughter by publishing photographs of people holding up wedge-tailed eagles which have been shot. There are few areas in Australia where these beautiful birds are safe from human depredation."

PERMANENT BUILDING SOCIETIES

The Permanent Building Societies were relatively young in the field of housing finance, and were providing a welcome alternative to the strict rules of the banks. But some of the provisions they had to face, as a legacy from the oligopoly of the banks, were still evident.

In a long Letter, a man talks about conscientiously saving for years to accumulate a deposit on a dwelling, and how his wife had also worked steadily to get that total.

However, he says, the Building Societies (and the banks) will not take into consideration his wife's income unless the wife produces **a medical certificate that she is incapable of having further children**.

"Apart from confronting a woman with this indignity, it is incredible that, in this age of the Pill, such 19th Century attitudes can prevail." He urges that the Societies accept the fact that people who are capable of raising a large deposit will also be wise enough and frugal enough to meet the repayments.

OCTOBER NEWS ITEMS

Dog-owners all over NSW **jammed** Council chambers today to get their dogs registered. From tomorrow, **unregistered** dogs will be impounded and **destroyed after one week**. Registered dogs will be kept for two weeks.

October 3rd. **The Brits have demos too.** The Prime Minister, Harold Wilson, was due to lead the service at a quiet church at England's seaside Brighton today. When he came to read the Bible, hundreds of student demonstrators invaded the Church and **enjoyed an old-fashioned riot**.... Shouting slogans that included "Murderer, Vietnam slaughter, and hypocrite", they lay down in the pews, preached an alternative sermon, and jostled some worthy citizens. At first glance, **it seems a bit hard on Wilson, because the Brits have not supported the Vietnam intervention**. Rioters said that it was not an action against Wilson personally, but just a more general publicity stunt against the war.

October 4th. **Signs of an evolving society.** The nation had its **second TAB agency robbery, netting over $10,000 last night**. A Sydney TAB operator was robbed at gunpoint. An earlier robbery, two months ago, had taken only $8,000. As a policeman said, robbers could be **expected to improve their technique as they get more experience**.

It looks like President Johnson will visit Australia for three days from October 20th. If he does come, **he might well get a warm welcom**e. I will cover the visit later in this Chapter.

October 9th. The (Sydney) *Sun-Herald* proudly announced that its 168-page issue **was the biggest-ever issue of**

an Australian newspaper. On Page Two, it carried the description of the annual Waratah Festival held on Saturday. A crowd of 750,000 crammed the streets, and it was described as Sydney's **gay** parade. No, No .... it just meant **happy**.

City Beaches across the nation are having trouble with **surf-board riders bashing into body surfers**. It seems likely that **separate lanes will be introduced**. Riders are objecting to this because they want to ride at **the exact best spot**, and not at some pre-determined lane that does not change with the sea's variations. The question is being asked as to **what powers do Councils have** in this matter.

The Australian cricket team will leave soon for South Africa. Last season, **the sensation of the game was a young lad called Doug Walter**s. But he will not go to South Africa with the rest of the team. He **is currently doing his National Service** in a military camp and is thus not available for selection. **He will not go to Vietnam either** because his birthday missed out in Lindsay Hassett's lottery draw.

September 18th. Hollywood **actor Clifton Webb died** in his home last night. He starred in such popular hits as *Cheaper by the Dozen*, and *Three Coins in a Fountain*.

September 19th. The spate of **armed robberies of Sydney's banks continues**. Yesterday, the staff of a major city Branch were met at entry, directed at gun-point to a vault, and **tied up hand and foot, blindfolded and gagged. The entire staff of 11 were treated thus**. The thieves escaped with $19,000. It took the staff ten minutes to get free and raise the alarm.

VIETNAM: CONSCIENTIOUS OBJECTORS

Whenever we get into a war, some of our citizens support the conscription of young men, and others oppose it. Even in the two World Wars, when patriotic fervour for fighting against Germany was extremely high, the issue of conscription divided the nation. Later, in the Korean War and now in Vietnam, when half the population were not convinced that we should be fighting at all, the enforcement of conscription was bound to cause much public dissent.

So, it is not surprising to find that a number of lads called up to service did not want to go to war. Many ruses were adopted to opt out, some of them legitimate, and many not. For example, it was not too hard to fail the medical exam, or to invent dying relatives who needed constant attention. Committees were set up round the nation to adjudicate appeals for exemption, and many quite suitable youths thus escaped the clutches of the Army. Also, many did not.

One avenue of escape was to claim a **conscientious** objection to military service. Put simply, because of religious or other convictions, the applicant had a material objection to fighting a war or to killing others. It was a matter of conscience. In order to make such a claim, the applicant often had to establish that he had been deeply religious for a long time, and that he thus had a high regard for human life.

If the person was successfully excused combat duty, he was still drafted. He was generally not sent overseas, but kept in the Army doing dogsbody work persistently. The worst feature for him was that the other soldiers regarded him as a "conscie", and as nothing better than a coward. Even after he left the military, and returned to the general community, the derogatory "conscie" followed him for many years. Not as bad as "scab", but a really nasty problem.

There was a lot of correspondence about these men, both the genuine ones and the fakes. I have included one that gives a moderate view of the attitudes of some people.

Letters, L C Masterman. By what right does William Yeo seek to minimise the integrity of **conscientious objectors**? He is reported to have said that "99 per cent of them are not bona fide." It is put forward without evidence, and is not supported by the facts. The further statement that "**even the lowest forms of animal life will fight for their homes and kids**" is an imputation of cowardice that is scandalous.

These youths have chosen a course requiring the highest degree of moral courage: the battle for civilisation and a rule of law in international affairs dictated by their consciences. I have watched the passage of many of them through the courts where they are examined and cross-examined by legal practitioners with a zeal resembling criminal prosecutions. I have met and talked with them, and listened to their endless self-questioning.

The published statistics show that between 20 and 50 per cent in the various States have been adjudged bona fide. Sir William's analysis of the integrity of the young conscientious objectors is far astray.

Comment. Figures made available about a year later said that about 36 per cent of applicants were thought to be legitimate. So they were granted a dispensation. It is they who became conscies. The ones who were refused exemptions might have found other ways out of service, or might have gone reluctantly into the forces.

JOHNSON'S VISIT AND VIETNAM

As soon as Johnson announced that he would visit Australia, we started to get the normal excited **headlines**. His security people said **he would be safe**. Because the President was staying 3 nights in Canberra, Holt would have to charter an airliner to take him to somewhere to meet someone. NSW would invite 1,000 guests to a reception at the Art Gallery. Johnson will spend four hours in Sydney. Free travel for all NSW children (to Sydney) to see the great man. The NSW Government will issue 100,000 free bi-flags (one each of Australia and US flags) to children along the route of the procession. As well, they will issue 100,000 lapel badges to the lucky children. A million strips of paper, 8 inches by 1 inch, will be given to office workers to throw during the ticker-tape procession. They will carry the message *"Hip, Hip, Hooray, for LBJ"*. **All very exciting, I think you will agree.**

As well as that, all police leave will be cancelled for the visit and 16 bands will enliven the route of the Sydney march. A floral display will be mounted at the Art Gallery.

By the 20th, he was on his way. He was greeted at Honolulu by grass-skirted hula dancers, and the headlines said that rain threatened as he was approaching Canberra. He landed and shook hands "impromptu" with spectators en route, had "informal" stops along his routes, delivered "unscheduled" speeches to cheering crowds, and had an "unplanned" evening meal with the Prime Minister at the Lodge. Fortunately, there were enough left-overs at the Lodge to feed him and his intimate party of 12. Demonstrators against Vietnam were kept well away from him.

Melbourne turned out for him next day, with a crowd of 500,000 cheering and waving. Demonstrators were again kept away, but security slipped a little when two paint bombs landed on his car, and blotted out the windscreen. His security men were speckled, but he stayed his immaculate self.

In Sydney, he ate and shook more hands, went on a wild ride through the city, a few children caught a glimpse of him, and he said some nice things. Anti-Vietnam demonstrators lay in front his car, the Premier told the driver to "run over the bastards", and they were dragged away.

On the way back to Manila, he told a crowd of 45,000 at Townsville that he knew some people disagreed with him on Vietnam, but he had seen on his visit that he was widely supported by the Australian public.

Correspondence on the visit was voluminous. There was widespread criticism of the amount of money spent on bringing children to Sydney, and giving them flags and so on. Much of this criticism dwelt on the number of other uses the money could be used for. This Letter is typical.

Letters, Brion E Bradshaw. How inconsistent is Mr Askin's plea of lack of money to assist the needy; the economic necessity of increased fares, hospital fees, stamp duty, etc., on the one hand, and on the other his provision of an "open cheque" to the Citizens' Special Welcoming Committee to President Johnson to provide paper flags, badges, banners and addressed streamers, all of which must inevitably finish in the gutter.

Let us not overlook the importance of such a historic visit, but let us spend our money in a more mature fashion, maybe on equipment for a hospital that will benefit and remind the community for years to come.

Some of it went a bit deeper.

Letters, Roberta Garrett. I write as an American citizen married to an Australian. My children were born here, I consider Australia my home, though I admit to being an unrepentant Yankee at heart, and a registered Democrat. I even cast my absentee ballot for LBJ.

But, really, must Sydney prostrate itself at the feet of Johnson?

After all, America is not heaven, nor is LBJ a god. Surely, to cite only one example, our money would be better spent, and, in the long run, our world image enhanced, if we would hand our children more library books and other essential tools of learning, instead of free flags and streamers saying, "hip, hip, hooray!"

Can't we tip our collective hats politely and get on with the job of developing independent thought and leadership?

Other writers were supportive of Johnson, Askin and Holt.

Letters, R V Cameron. I am appalled at the churlish attitude of some of your correspondents with respect to the money being spent in NSW to make President Johnson and his wife welcome.

If the requirements of hospitality and a sense of the historic nature of the occasion make no appeal to these people, perhaps crude commercial considerations of self-interest may.

For the expenditure of a few thousand dollars on transport concessions, flags and entertainment at the Art Gallery, NSW may expect favourable publicity overseas through the Press and television worth scores of millions. It is difficult to estimate the impetus the Johnson visit will give to the tourist trade alone, but it is sure to be considerable.

I am sure the majority of citizens of the State will congratulate the Askin Government and the Citizens' Welcoming Committee on the steps they have taken to make the visit of the United States President a memorable one.

There was also a lot of criticism of the speed at which the motorcade went. No one on the roadside had the chance to see Johnson at all. The minders said that this was from fear of another Kennedy-style shooting by a sniper, and this was probably the case. Though some families said that if they had known this in advance, they would not have travelled from Wilcannia.

There were lots of other Letters. Some people worried about children being hurt if the demonstrations grew into a riot. Some dobbed in a few students who threw a stone at the motorcade. Others said that demonstrators should know when to do their thing, but it was rudeness to do it when the President of the US was here. Someone replied that the same great man is killing thousands of children in Vietnam, and he should be able to take a bit of rudeness.

A NEW DEAL FOR INDONESIA

As Australians, we do not look overseas all that often. In general, we are happy with our lot here, and problems in other parts of the world are not at the top of our discussions at the Sunday barbie.

Now, of course, that insularity is being shattered by events in Vietnam. Also, Rhodesia is getting more mentions than it had previously. A third country, Indonesia, is also coming into our consciousness, though in this case, the news is more benign than in the other two countries.

I mentioned earlier that Malaya and Indonesia appeared to have settled their differences, and had laid down their arms. Well, surprising to some, the situation has improved and a genuine peace has broken out between the two nations. This means that the fears that some persons were nursing have given way to more constructive matters.

For example, some commentators had been fearing that the devout Muslim community of Indonesia would align itself with the atheistic Reds. Others had thought that the nasty Indonesians would use West New Guinea as a base from which to take over East New Guinea. Such people had now been silenced, and instead the Letters are more constructive and certainly more friendly to Indonesia.

Letters, W B Donnolley. If Australians are serious about building good relations with Indonesia, they should take immediate action to relieve the tragic famine on the island of Lombok. According to Dr R Bain Usef, provincial health director for the area, there may be 80,000 dead from hunger on Lombok by January.

Now that our own drought problem has been somewhat relieved, we could well afford to show some practical consideration for our less fortunate neighbours.

Our Federal Government has shown that it is not afraid **to spend millions destroying lives in Vietnam**. Why not divert some of our national income towards saving the lives of undernourished and impoverished children only 1,100 miles away?

A dozen other writers said virtually the same thing.

KEEPING FIT

In the 50-plus years since 1966, Australia has gradually convinced itself that it needs to get fit. For example, the jogging craze is still with us, the number of gym memberships has multiplied enormously, pilates is an epidemic, a six-pack under the ribs is mandatory for some unfortunate young men. Fitness is big business now, more so than ever before.

Back in 1966, though, women's magazines were trying to exploit the healthy-living craze. *The Woman's Weekly*, for example, had article after article on such things as heathy diet and related weight loss. The mantra was to eat good sensible food, not much of it, and do a fair bit of exercise.

This 1966 Letter below sets it out rather nicely.

Letters, (Mrs) F P Ory. I agree that most people indulge in too much food, drink, TV, &c., then complain of ill-health or overweight.

Mr Mullen did not exaggerate the daily intake of foods he listed for an average Australian. Most housewives seem more concerned about buying the largest packet of pre-packed food for the least money and not caring for its food value.

I buy most of my provisions loose from a health store. Sometimes it even costs more, but I know the nutritive value is more, and it doesn't need any additives to make it taste good.

When my friends know what I eat, they ask why I am on a "diet." I reply, "My daily food intake is not a 'diet,' merely – healthy eating." I eat no bread or potatoes, drink only black tea or coffee, with brown sugar.

Breakfast: Boiled egg, glass of milk, fresh fruit.

Lunch: Cheese, lean meat, salad, crispbreads, glass of milk.

Dinner: Lean meat or fish, vegetables, salad, glass of water. Nothing between meals. (The stomach needs a rest.)

I retire early, rise early and can't bear the windows closed, except when it is foggy. I feel fighting fit, never tire, seldom get a bad cold, and I am always "on the go." I cycle everywhere. "More 'Bikes' and Less Food" should be the motto, for a healthy nation.

Comment. Mrs Ory did not have the benefits of the current fads for things like vitamin supplements, and yoghurts, and colonic irrigation, and caveman diets, and protein shakes, and the like, hers is a simple regime that she can stick to.

I often wonder at the fads that have come, and gone, over the years, and whether any advanced routines have achieved material benefits. In fact, I sometimes wonder whether some of them have done more harm that good. I suspect that, living in a world of vested interest and hyper marketing, I will never know for sure.

Another comment. Oh Dear! I must be getting old. I am so cynical at times.

LETTERS IN BRIEF

No war toys. A Melbourne toy manufacturer is donating over 15,000 toys to Vietnam for distribution by Aussie troops to children there for Christmas. They will include dolls, water pistols, whistling train engines, boats, beach buckets and spades. The Army and Department of Supply are co-operating, and have men working overtime packing the goods into shipping containers.

Firearms for all. There was talk about restricting the sale of firearms in several States. The present rules were lenient, and most often consisted of applying for a licence for a rifle, waiting for two weeks while the police did a rough check on you, then collecting the licence, and buying at the local gunsmith. The police checks were of course not computerised, and were only on criminal records of major crimes.

There was quite a lot of support for some change to regulations, but it was far from overwhelming. This Letter is typical of the opposition.

Letters, T Prosser, Bellevue Hill. Control of firearms by legislative action never has been and probably never will be effective. Criminals, and others, will obtain firearms as long as small-arms factories exist. A determined man can make a "gun" in his home workshop with or without a lathe. Licensing of pistols and revolvers has only made these items more expensive to obtain illegally.

No police force however dedicated can protect the public 24 hours a day. Many private citizens and their wives feel much safer with a shotgun in their homes as protection against the hooligans brazen enough to knock on a front door and then force their way in to the terror of women and children. Criminals are no doubt delighted at the prospect of a defenseless public. They could probably obtain a reduction on their insurance premium as the "occupation" would be less hazardous.

The answer to the current crime wave could easily lie in the opposite direction, **more guns in more hands with a shot or two at the armed bandits**.

NOVEMBER NEWS ITEMS

Pastoralists in the Northern Territory will, from November 1st, have to pay **Aboriginal employees** on their stations a **much increased minimum wage**. They will also need to provide accommodation for the employees and their families that meet minimum standards....

Dwellings will need to have windows, walls 9ft high, flooring (of stone, concrete or wood), and weather-proof roofs. Authorities point out that many stations do provide these facilities already, and they aim to improve conditions over the next years so that **all** employees will benefit....

Comment. It might seem that to have **a home that is rain-proof is scarcely good enough**, but these provisions taken with a big increase in wages, represent **a much improved status for these Aborigines. The worry** is that some pastoralists might say that the extra costs impose too big a burden on them, and sack some workers.

First Tuesday in November. Galilee, the horse and not the astronomer, won by two lengths.

A lioness, two years old, was at the bottom of the pecking order in Melbourne zoo. **A male lion knocked her over with his paw, and killed her with a bite above the heart**, and dragged her to his den. There he stood over her and refused to move. **The incident was witnessed by dozens of children, and was filmed by a Channel 7 cameraman** who happened to be there at the time.

Politicians are starting to campaign seriously for **the Federal elections to be held on November 26th.** Political meetings are drawing **much bigger crowds than in the decade since the introduction of TV**. A few have ended in punch ups and some pushing and shoving over Vietnam issues. Nothing serious.

In the Indian city of Delhi, a Hindu demonstration against the **killing of cows** turned ugly and developed into a riot. Ten people were killed and 200 wounded. In the riot, hundreds of screaming holy men, some of them naked, tried to lead a crowd of thousands into storming the Parliament building. The rioting was city wide, and a two-night full curfew has been imposed on the city.

The population of Sydney has reached two and a half million. Melbourne has 2.1 million.

November 25th. Australia had its **first TV link to Britain via satellite today**. The receptor in Australia was a large TV dish at **Carnarvon** on the north-west coast of Western Australia. 700 locals gathered to watch the event. It is hoped that Australia will be linked to major cities in the world in the next two years. In particular, it is hoped that **some direct broadcasts can be made from the Mexico Olympic Games in 1968**.

The Prime Minister and the Liberal Party had a crushing victory in the elections. Its new majority will be a record. The defeat of Labor means the **resignation of the Labor leader, Calwell**. That's what he said, anyway....

Now **Holt** gets a mandate to continue with his involvement in Vietnam. He also had a sensible election package of limited aid for non-state schools. **Calwell**, on the other hand, fought almost entirely on the conscription issue, and while he gained the support of lots of parents, he had no other policy of note to stand on. He suffered a large drop in votes cast for him personally.

VIETNAM AND MR WHITE

William White was a 21-year-old new school teacher from an inner Sydney suburb. Over the previous year he had **refused to register** for National Service on the grounds that he was a conscientious objector, and refused to be bound by any laws or regulation pertaining to armed service. As a consequence, he **had been fired from his position of teacher**, and was now appearing before the Special Federal Court for failing to comply with a call-up notice. He was committed to the custody of a major in the Army's Far Eastern Command. The major attempted to serve him with papers ordering him to turn up at barracks the next day. White refused to accept them.

White said at the time "I have no intention of co-operating with Army authorities." For the next three days he waited for the Army's reaction, during which time Arthur Calwell said that if Labor won the upcoming election, then White would be absolved of any offence he was deemed to have committed.

After three days, nine uniformed officers and four detectives from the NSW Police Force were on his doorstep. It was they, rather than military police, who came to arrest him because the latter were not permitted to enter houses. The four detectives seemed to be the largest quartet that could be found, and they dragged him off in full view of TV cameras and dozens of newspaper photographers. It made headlines in all news outlets in the nation.

Comment. Photographs of White being dragged away became famous, and were used for years by anti-conscription groups to stir passions.

Controversy over conscies, never small, grew much larger. Sympathy for White was strong. After all, he was clearly not some yobbo or beatnik, he had recently had a respectable job.

Further, the argument against most applicants for objection status was that they were not sincere. There was no doubt at all **that this man was sincere**. "I will never take part in military service."

The Editor of the *SMH* chimed in. He argued that if **White's** application was rejected, then surely **all** cases must be rejected, and there was no point in having hearings. He went on to say that the local magistrate who heard his application in the first place was not equipped to make such complex decisions of conscience, and that a dedicated panel should hear the more serious applications.

At this stage, a number of writers made their various comments to the newspapers.

Letters, George Brown, Sydney Tech High School P and C Association. Congratulations on your forthright editorial commenting on the conscription of William White, a trained schoolteacher.

One of the most vital points of this issue is being overlooked. Last week the newspapers carried an advertisement with the appealing headline "Come Back to Teaching" while, on the other hand, trained teachers are being conscripted on completion of their training. The teacher shortage – particularly in secondary schools – is so desperate that the Department of Education is prepared to recruit teachers from graduates who are untrained in teaching methods and, without this training, some will never be capable of teaching successfully.

The fact that the Education Department will – and does – employ untrained (and often, unsuitable) graduates and yet allows this capable teacher to spend two years in the Army (against his will and conscience) for a civil offence must only add to the already mounting chaos of the Wyndham scheme.

I feel that it is imperative that every P and C association, every district council and every parent speak up now on matters vitally affecting the education of our children.

Letters, Garry F Spring. It is many years since I have heard quoted or seen recorded the introduction by Abraham Lincoln in 1863 to the Draft Bill. The present seems an appropriate time to declaim it as a lesson for all Australians. It reads:

"**Voluntaryism** is the unprincipled dodge of cowardly politicians. It has ground the choicest seed corn of the nation. It has consumed the young, the generous, the intelligent, the brave. It has wasted the best moral, social and political elements of the Republic and left **the cowards, the shirkers and the moneymakers to stay at home and procreate their kind.**"

In case it may be suggested that I have no sons liable to serve, I add that my elder is in the present draft. He and I are proud of the country that calls him and he is proud to serve it.

Letters, E B Mowbray. Twice in 50 years men of this country have fought for national and personal freedom. This freedom is now denied in our own country to conscientious objectors. No constructive alternative is provided. Surely the Government will discontinue this policy which is opposed to the freedoms we have continually upheld.

None of these efforts helped White. He was taken to Watson's Bay, en route to an Army base outside Wagga. He was fined $10 and five days loss of pay. An Army spokesman said that "this disposes of any charges against him." But that was probably wishful thinking, because White was still in his civvy clothes, and refusing to accept standard military uniform or equipment.

As these events proceeded, more Letters were inspired, and these two stand out. The first is because it was a constructive suggestion that might work if our world was a different one. The second, beautifully written, should not go to waste if only because of the clarity of its attack on the Governmet.

Letters, David Taylor. We wonder if the Government could consider the formation of an Australian "peace corps" in which overseas service, unlike that in the American peace corps, might be accepted as an alternative form of National Service?

Australia does send each year, of course, a small number of "Australian Volunteers Abroad." Unfortunately, few young men eligible for National Service have been able, because of their youth, to obtain the academic qualifications necessary for this work.

Is there any sensible reason why the Government should not offer an alternative, apart from the present somewhat limited possibilities of either military service or military detention, to conscientious objectors as responsible as William White?

The Government must surely realise the advantages in giving these people the opportunity at least of offering their abilities to work among the masses in the underdeveloped Asian countries.

Mao and Ho, we believe, encourage some of their young intellectuals to work discreetly in the villages of Laos, Cambodia, Thailand, Burma and Vietnam. Why is it then that we are not doing the same?

The second Letter was from Allan Ashbolt, representing the views of the Ex-Services Association of Australia. He states that the Government, through its prosecution of Bill White, was attacking the liberties of all Australians.

Firstly, he said, our war in Vietnam is undeclared, and the enemy is not even defined. To take young men, and force them to fight, is to adopt the same practices as were used with the 18th Century pressgangs.

Secondly, the Govenment is punishing persons who are reluctant killers, and in so doing is abandoning all forms of compassion and tolerance, and instead introducing sadism and fanaticism.

Thirdly, the demand for subservience from its citizens is the same doctrine of blind obedience that was made by Hitler's regime when it forced good people to do the most outrageous acts against their will.

Fourthly, the Government speaks of stopping aggresion, but at the same time it is committing aggression against its own people. This is a denial of the moral values on which all decent societies are based.

Ashbolt concluded his Letter by referring to the specific injustices handed out to Bill White, but he goes on to aver that the policies being implemented by the Government are a threat to all Australians and to Australia's development as a free community. "It will be further evidence that the dark shadow of authoritarianism is moving over us all."

Comment. I remind you that Allan Ashbolt was the same person who impetuously jumped onto the stage at a demo in February.

Now that since White had "joined" the Army, most news of him was censored. We found out that, after 10 days, he had refused to accept a uniform, and refused to accept equipment, and refused to sign military documents. He had been charged on each of these accounts. He was being confined to his cell, and was under 24-hour guard.

Comment. At this point, it looked like White had disappeared from view for the duration. But, as it turned out, that was not

the case. **There was further news of him on December 23ʳᵈ.**
I wonder what it will be.

THE PLACE OF ZOOS

Dr Heini Hediger, a Swiss expert brought to Australia to comment on Sydney's Taronga Park Zoo, presented a very critical report. He said it had many badly designed structures, that some species were over-crowded, and mortality rates were abnormally high for others.

He also referred to the fact that over 100 creatures of all types were killed for food, or killed and burned, last year. (This was partly because the zoo was overstocked on wedge-tail eagles, but quarantine and Customs regulations stopped their sale and export overseas.)

A second report a few days later pointed out some other bad features. It was from a Dr Brattstrom, from California State University.

Letters, (Dr) Bayard Brattstrom, Professor of Zoology, California State College. The things that struck me most were: Overcrowding (animals and cages), no general organisation (marsupials in several places), overstocking of some forms (tree kangaroos, pigeons, etc.), cement floors (for kangaroos), reptile cages with so many rocks and plants that people can't see the reptiles, diseased skin (albino buffalo), too many bars, wires, ugly cement walls, too few and usually inaccurate signs (for people as well as on cages), poor and expensive food for people, poor feeding of animals (food usually just thrown in cages, often hitting animals in face – e.g., kangaroos), an inadequate aquarium.

This hit Sydney where it hurt a lot. Everyone knew that the zoo was running on a shoestring, and survived only by the benevolence of the philanthropist, Sir Edward Hallstrom.

Residents of Sydney, and a million visitors over the years, placed Taronga Zoo high in their regard. They saw the beasts and creatures, in a wonderful location, and a day out at the zoo was an institution that many people treasured. To have the zoo criticised, and also Sir Edward, came as a shock

Letters, Bruce H Dalton. "A day at the zoo" has been a traditional and delightful treat for children for many years. We of the older generation have noted with distress that over the years it has deteriorated. The exciting tram trip up the hill has been replaced by a smelly diesel bus; the general condition of the zoo has become shabby.

But we rightly blame the financial neglect of successive State Governments, and it is simply shocking that a man like the honorary director, Sir Edward Hallstrom, should be criticised or blamed in any way at all. It is not necessary to repeat what he has done to keep the zoo going, it is well known to all Sydneysiders, who respect and honour him for it. We hope he will not be too hurt by the self-interested criticisms of the few, but will remember that he has a place in the hearts of the people, the little people of this city, which many politicians and "professionals" must envy.

Indeed, it seems Sir Edward's greatest sin is to be an enthusiastic amateur rather than a professional. As one who has suffered much at the hands of professional painters, plumbers, motor mechanic, engineers and even physicians, I respectfully submit that what we need today is the good old enthusiastic amateur, trained at his own expense, willing to devote more time to his craft than money can pay for. Many of the old-time doctors and tradesmen of all kinds were like this; today many, but not all, professionals are in the game for what they can get out of it.

The care of animals is a Labor of love, and in such matters, especially, the enthusiastic amateur is much to be preferred to the professional.

Writers from across the nation sprang to defend Sir Edward.

Letters, (Mrs) L Ollif. I am shocked at the unnecessary embarrassment caused a great Australian after he has devoted a quarter-century of time and effort to Taronga Park Zoo. Surely such an inquiry was not necessary during his lifetime, at least.

Seemingly, any passing visitor, whether qualified or not, has only to criticise one of our institutions, and immediately an overseas "expert" will be called in to improve it. No doubt Dr Hediger felt that, as he was brought here to offer criticism, he had to do so, but it would seem that his suggestions are relatively minor, and may or may not be of value.

As a world traveller who has visited many zoos, I would say that the only one I have seen even approaching ours is that outside Kandy, in Ceylon. If there is a better one, I've yet to hear of it – and don't mention Whipsnade or Regent's Park. When I visited the former, admittedly some years ago, it was a vast tract of land, with large enclosures and very few animals. One could walk a quarter-mile and see half a dozen deer.

At the opposite end of the scale was Regent's Park, with a close huddle of small cages holding mouldy-looking animals. Even their much-vaunted polar bears were in small concrete pits, with no visible facilities, and were a grey colour.

The advice of one of the many thousands who appreciate what Sir Edward has done is – let's spend our surplus public money on the Opera House and leave the zoo to Sir Edward, who, practically unaided, has done a very good job there.

Letters, (Mrs) Ruth Phillips. In the first place, I don't think a foreigner from the cold European climate of Zurich would be as gifted or as experienced as our very own Sir Edward Hallstrom, who for 25 years has put everything into our Taronga Park. I have seen many zoos on my world travels, including Zurich, and nothing comes up to Taronga Park.

For goodness' sake let Australia have her own experts deal with our own country. We run rings around the overseas views because we know our own country better than outsiders.

Personal comment. I too held Sir Edward in high esteem. **Firstly**, because my family and I had spent a number of great days at the zoo as our youngsters got to the right age. I, perhaps naively, thought it was world class. **Secondly**, because my eldest brother had worked in Sir Edward's Silent Knight Refrigerator factory for years. According to my brother, Sir Edward was a most intelligent and benevolent employer.

Sir Edward pointed out that it was **his** money, and **not** the money from the State or the Commonwealth, that was keeping the zoo going. Again, he received much support from the public on this matter.

Still, there were people who saw it all differently.

Letters, H Fitzgerald. It is time zoos were abolished. They are little more than animal prisons at best, involving passive cruelty always. Creatures from totally different environments, such as the polar regions in the case of Australian zoos, must suffer greatly for much of the year. The same applies to exporting our animals to very cold climate countries.

The only justification offered is the negligible "educational value" of seeing creatures living out their miserable existence in artificial conditions. This can be better achieved from films made in the natural habitat.

Cease breeding to perpetuate the vicious system and let all zoos be done away with as soon as practicable.

Letters, (Miss) Diana Rawlinson. While I have great respect for the work of Sir Edward Hallstrom, he does admit that Taronga Park Zoo could be improved and surely lack of funds is no excuse for making animals suffer. If animals cannot be provided with a reasonable replica of their natural surroundings, they should be either freed or, if this is not practical, given a humane death.

I agree in principle with H Fitzgerald, but I do not think that zoos should be abolished since they can provide both entertainment and education. Also, natural habitats in the wild are becoming far too few and far between to enable the abolition of zoos.

But an animal in unnatural surroundings that cannot show off all its behavioural characteristics is not content, and is neither educational nor a joy to watch.

Comment. Gradually, Taronga Park became less dependent on Sir Edward, and more money was found in the public purse. The criticisms above were in fact heeded over the years, and now it rates, along with several zoos in other Capital cities, very high by any sort of standards that are set.

DECEMBER NEWS ITEMS

A vagrant was arrested in Canberra today because he had a loaded gun **and intended to kill Prime Minister Holt**. His reason was a general resentment against society, and was not related to Vietnam. "I had **a photo of Holt** because I wanted to ensure **that I fired at the right man**."

The NSW Government **in principle** agreed **to compensate victims of crimes**, rather than have the perpetrator do this. This was a **most advanced legal concept**, and would take some time to implement. At this stage, the money paid would be only small, but it would be granted **as a legal right**. The compensation, on a fixed scale, would be paid whether or not the offender was arrested.

45 gravediggers and workers at Botany Cemetery held a snap strike from 9.30 am yesterday. This meant that half a dozen sets of **early mourners were compelled to move coffins into graves, and then fill in the graves**. Later funerals were delayed until tomorrow, as were all cremations. The distress caused was considerable. The workers proposed to return to work tomorrow.

The NSW Government moved further into the 20th Century by allowing **liquor merchants to sell spirits and liquor and beer by the single bottle.** Previously, this was illegal, so that if you wanted a bottle of Scotch, you needed to buy a dozen bottles.

There are currently **five nations with the capacity to develop nuclear bombs.** The US, Britain, Russia, France and China. Believe it or not, these five have got together and agreed on something. Not only that, it was something sensible. They agreed that **all nuclear testing in outer** space should be banned in future. Also, **all claims to sovereignty to any part of space would be banned.** To the best of my knowledge, all parties have stuck to the agreement. This is not a common event.

December 13th. **Francis Chichester**, a British yachtsman, sailed into Sydney. He **had sailed round the world single-handed** from Plymouth via the clipper route. He was the first man to do this. He took 107 days. A few days later, he continued on westward and finished his **round-the-world trip** in record time. He was knighted soon after.

December 16th. It was reliably reported that **the number of Australian troops in Vietnam** will be increased from the current **4,500 to 6,000.** Plus 1,000 airmen.

For decades, the waterside workers have had a bad **reputation for striking.** It appears that they are currently working on agreements with the stevedoring companies that will reduce the strikes. It is proposed that they be **given permanent employment**, rather than the current piece-work and roster. Also, that **redundancy payments** be made when **automation** takes effect.

Here's news for punters. Bookmakers on some tracks round Australia will now be allowed to **bet each-way**.

December 20th. **Three Aboriginal men were killed instantly** by a passing vehicle near the NSW town of Condobolin while they were **changing a tyre** near the edge of the road. A 27-year-old man was charged..

TV's Man From U.N.C.L.E. **has arrived in Australia. Robert Vaughan was met by 1,000 fans** at Mascot airport in a rousing reception. He said he has killed about 1,000 villains on screen, and gets about $10,000 for each episode.

1966 AMERICAN FILMS

THE BIBLE	RICHARD HARRIS
	AVA GARDNER
HAWAII	RICHARD HARRIS
	JULIE ANDREWS
VIRGINIA WOOLF	ELIZABETH TAYLOR**
	RICHARD BURTON
SAND PEBBLES	STEVE McQUEEN
	CANDICE BERGEN
MAN FOR ALL SEASONS	PAUL SCHOFIELD*
	WENDY HILLER
GOOD, BAD, AND UGLY	CLINT EASTWOOD
	ELI WALLACH
LT ROBIN CRUSOE USN	DICK VAN DYKE
	NANCY KWAN
GRAND PRIX	JAMES GARNER
	EVA MARIE SAINT
THE PROFESSIONALS	BURT LANCASTER
	LEE MARVIN
ALFIE	MICHAEL CAINE
	SHELLEY WINTERS

ACADEMY AWARDS

BEST MOVIE:	A MAN FOR ALL SEASONS
BEST ACTOR:	PAUL SCHOFIELD*
BEST ACTRESS:	ELIZABETH TAYLOR**

TOP OF POPS

BOOTS ARE FOR WALKING	NANCY SINATRA
WE CAN WORK IT OUT	THE BEATLES
YELLOW SUBMARINE	THE BEATLES
HITCH HIKER	BOBBY, LAURIE
SOMEWHERE MY LOVE	RAY CONNIFF
LADY GODIVER	PETER, GORDON
OOH LA LA	NORMIE ROWE
STEP BACK	JOHNNY YOUNG
FRIDAY ON MY MIND	THE EASYBEATS
STRANGERS IN THE NIGHT	FRANK SINATRA
PAINT IT BLACK	ROLLING STONES
GOOD	BEACH BOYS
BORN FREE	MATT MONROE
WILD THING	THE TROGGS
SPICKS AND SPECKS	BEE GEES
SORRY	THE EASYBEATS
AS TEARS GO BY	ROLLING STONES
19th CENTURY BREAKDOWN	ROLLING STONES

MR WHITE AND VIETNAM

December 23rd. **Remember William White**, the so-called draft dodger? He disappeared under army camouflage for a month, and emerged into the Sydney Court of Petty Sessions, before a single magistrate. He was questioned for some four hours about his adventures and motives. He said that at one stage as a lad he had accidentally killed a bird with a catapult. "I was immensely shocked, I went over to the bird and its neck was broken, but it was in pain and I knew it would soon die. I took a rock, and hit the bird on the head to kill it quickly." From this, he realised the suffering that violence could bring, and it became a part of his thinking.

The magistrate concluded that his beliefs were immature, but he was quite sincere. "He does have a conscientious belief, and I intend to grant his application." That meant that he was excused from military service, and he was free to go.

He was due to get married on January 9th, and he was soon to talk to the Education Department about getting his job back. The army was relieved because they had never wanted the publicity that the incidents had provoked. So, along with the cheering crowd in the Court, everyone can feel good at this happy ending.

CHINA'S INTENTIONS

China was the lightly sleeping giant. It was not sending hordes of troops into Vietnam, but **it too had advisors**, and was giving aircraft and supplies to the friendly North Vietnam state. Maybe some of these found their way to the Viet Cong.

In any case, it was not officially **in** the Vietnam conflict. Still, much of America's immense propaganda was directed against China and, rightly or wrongly, some of it affected opinion here. Let me give you a few Letters that show what was being said.

Letters, Michael Sheilds.   Kenneth Gee has missed the main point of my letter. I did not propose the seating of **two** Chinas in the United Nations, but advocated the entry of **mainland** China into the world body with the concurrent renaming of "Nationalist China" as Formosa.

The principal reason why China demands the expulsion of "Nationalist China" is a pre-condition of her entry is because Formosa, under the dictatorship of Chiang Kai-shek, is recognised as the sole voice of China. Surely the absurdity of this untenable position is indisputable.

As for Mr Gee's assertion that the Chinese Reds do not represent the Chinese people, I can only comment that his knowledge of China is sadly lacking.

Although I agree that the formation of the United Nations was designed to promote world peace, how can it do this effectively if it **ostracises a quarter of the world's population**? By deliberately isolating China now, we will only increase her bellicose attitude towards us.

Letters, B Mercier. Once Mao was in the saddle, any mention of Australia to the average Red Chinese official in Peking brought **the claim that Communist China would settle big numbers of her people here.**

In 1952, the Communist Chinese propaganda department exhibited in Peking streets enormous posters bearing maps of Australia and words triumphantly claiming that China would invade Australia and settle 50 million of her people in the centre of this continent. The posters said Australia had adopted a "dog-in-the-manger" attitude about Central Australia, which she had failed to develop, yet had denied it to others who would develop it. "We will irrigate this region so that it can support 50 million Chinese!" declared the posters.

When, in 1952, I applied to a police chief in Tientsin for an exit visa to Australia, he commented, when handing me the document: "one day we will meet there!"

Australians who treat lightly the threat of Communist invasion are playing with fire.

Letters, B C McKillop. In 1964, I was overseas on sabbatical leave, and in October travelled from Britain to Japan via Scandinavia and the Soviet Union. On the train between Helsinki and Leningrad I shared a compartment with two diplomats from Peking.

They were quite friendly, even offering me some of the food they had brought with them because there was no restaurant car. However, their attitude was very definite, and exactly like that described in Mr Mercier's letter. The elder of the two, who did most of the talking, told me that Australia was not being properly developed, and in particular Central Australia was shamefully neglected.

When I said that most of the land in question was too barren and lacking in water for closer settlement, he strongly disagreed. The Chinese, he said, had reclaimed vast areas of Central Asia that were just as barren, and if we couldn't or wouldn't develop our own inland areas, we ought to accept a few million Chinese settlers to do the job for us. Unless we did something of this kind he considered the Australians had no right to occupy Australia.

He was so definite and emphatic that I felt at the time that he must be echoing the party line, and Mr Mercier's letter confirms this probability.

Letters, Eric Aarons. I was in Peking throughout 1952, and saw no posters of any kind bearing maps of Australia, nor did I ever see or hear such words anywhere.

Letters, B Mercier.   Eric Aarons states that, unlike me, he did not see in Peking, in 1952, posters bearing maps of Australia and words proclaiming that China would invade Australia.

Presuming that, like me, he can read Chinese. I reply that there are none so blind as those who will not see. In 1953 a relative of mine in Peking wrote to me in Australia that the posters were still on show in that city.

Since you published my original letter about the posters on November 23, several former Peking residents, now living in NSW, have written to me saying that they well remember seeing the posters.

Comment.   Let us all hope, as we sit on the verge of 1967, that Red China keeps her cool, and stays out of direct and overt involvement in Vietnam. If it doesn't, we will regret it.

A QANTAS STRIKE

Qantas pilots staged a good strike in December. They managed to disrupt a lot of traffic worldwide during the month, and given that the Christmas rush was planned, none of them were too popular. What they wanted was more money, and better conditions and more say in running the business. This was a familiar theme among strikers. And of course, they won some of their demands just before the heaviest Christmas traffic. Again, a familiar end to a well-timed strike.

One good thing that came out of the strike was the perverse Letter that I have enclosed below.

Letters, J Hogan.   Regarding the Qantas dispute, it might be of interest to compare the wages and conditions in a transport industry of equal importance, and possibly greater magnitude, that is the Railways of NSW.

Where the Qantas captain who commands the multi-million-dollar Boeing jets, with a passenger capacity of 100, has been offered a salary of $15,000, commensurate with his knowledge, responsibilities and the value of the equipment with which he works, the driver of the multi-million-dollar glamour train, Southern Aurora, with a passenger capacity of 200, or the Spirit of Progress, with a capacity of almost 500, receives a base rate of $3,000 a year.

Another interesting comparison is in the field of accommodation when away from home. Where the Qantas flight crews, consistent with modern standards of living, are accommodated in first-class hotels, their railway counterparts must, by regulation, stay in departmental barracks.

In these barracks, where train crews spend up to 20 hours, no amenities are provided, radios are banned and the bedrooms, like the old-fashioned "bush pub," are provided with one bare 40-watt bulb. In peak periods, drivers and firemen/observers often have to wait for outgoing crews to vacate bedrooms before they can occupy them, making their own beds.

In barracks kitchens, where crews cook their own meals, hygiene standards are minimal, flies thrive in an ideal environment and the danger of hepatitis is ever present.

Why this disparity? Is it that the Government service has failed to keep pace with modern standards, or that flight crews, the glamour jobs, can command glamour salaries and conditions?

Comment. At a discussion night that I sometimes have with oldies, I asked for answers to Hogan's question. Nearly everyone said **initially** that the answer was that anyone can become an engine driver, and that only a few can become a pilot. When I came back to the question later, after a few chardonnays, opinions had switched, and my oldies now said that becoming a pilot was easy if you had money or knew the right people. From this, they concluded that while Australia might not have **a class system like Britain, based on land, history, and schools**, it does have an elite that is based on occupation and education and merit.

When I asked whether this was a good thing, those of the meritocracy said yes, and the others said no. But it was interesting that **all** of them mixed together freely, and **all** of them felt free to voice opinions.

My conclusion from **this sample of one**? Of course Australia has class distinctions. But to compare them to those of other nations, including Britain and the US, is to compare apples and oranges.

BLAME THE PRIVET

The months of December and January every year in Australia are different from the others. In those latter months, the media fill us up with scare stories, tell us of atrocities, and breed a feeling of dread for the future that we lap up, and convince ourselves that we are up with the news.

In December, the media know that we cannot be distracted from our Christmas shopping, and our parties, and our holiday planning. **In January**, they know that they cannot compete with the Davis Cup and cricket on TV, the lure of the tinnie and the fish hook, and of course the evening barbie at the holiday shack.

So, they go light on big and tragic news, and fill the paper with really interesting stuff. Often, they include a series of silly Letters that start with one innocent complaint, and then writers take up their pens and add comments for the month. Over the years, I have seen them extract the last breath out of such things as how to make tea, bread making, bread making with seaweed, flies in Bathurst, Christmas crowds, children on trains, railway refreshment rooms, and the lot.

So, here we are again, and I am happy to say that this time round the **culprit is privet**. Sometimes that little monster is momentarily tamed and shaped into grandma's hedge, but normally it lies in wait on the edge of streets and parks with its scratchy things out ready to scratch you.

One perceptive writer started the ball rolling.

Letters, Maisie Vester. During October and November each year I watch several women friends of mine suffer badly from hay fever and some asthma attacks. On investigation I find all have contact with the shrub privet – either in their gardens or their near neighbours.

In America this shrub is banned as a noxious weed. Here it is encouraged and Sydneysiders go down like ninepins with hay fever as soon as it starts to bud.

Why can't it be banned here?

Letters flooded in. They agreed that privet was a villain, especially in November and December when hay fever was at its worst. One perceptive gardener pointed out that blowflies are attracted to privet flowers, resulting in more of the filthy flies in homes. There were suggestions that New Zealand had banned it, but this was quickly denied by the NZ Trade Commissioner. A number of Councils were applauded for banning the menace, but these reports also proved to be wrong.

Inevitably, though, someone had a different idea. He deplored the plant-haters for their ill-informed highly imaginative ideas. He goes on to say:

Letters, N A McClellan. May I inform L M McLeod that the blowfly is not a nectar-gathering creature and has no interest in the flowers of the privet? I suggest that he learns to distinguish the blowfly from the dark races of honey-bee.

While I have sympathy for genuine hay-fever sufferers, can they not agree that it is better to treat the cause of hay fever, an allergy to pollen, rather than to destroy useful and attractive shrubs. As many scores of tress, shrubs and plants produce pollen in the late spring it is absurd to single out the privet for malediction. In fact, as the privet produces relatively little pollen, it is not at all likely that it contributes to hay fever.

Into the fray stepped a "manufacturer of spray for many years, who has an intimate knowledge of all walking, flying and crawling insects." He acknowledges that blowflies are not nectar-gathering, but "whatever their interest, I have seen them hovering around privet in bloom on many occasions in great numbers." Interesting, of course, but hardly decisive.

So, we go back to the main game. There is a reminder that the US bans privet as a noxious weed. "It is hardly likely that so forward a country would go to such lengths were this shrub not the Number One menace to hay fever and asthma sufferers." Some nark spoiled this thesis by pointing out that the US is made up of **many States**, and that each of them makes their own policy on noxious weeds. It might be that a few of them ban privet, but to say that **the entire US** bans it is a gross exaggeration.

The final word went to a real authority.

Letters, Lenley I Mackay, Noxious Weed Inspector, Walcha Shire Council. I have watched closely the progress of the privet along roadsides and watercourses in almost every coastal shire from Gloucester to the border, spread on to more useful land where it now covers thousands of acres.

The Nambucca, Bellingen, Tintenba, Tenania and Tomki shires have shown an alarming rate of spread over the last five years.

We have experienced the introduction and subsequent spread of lantana, groundsell bush and Crofton weed and in my opinion privet will rival these as aggressive plants. I draw the attention of the Noxious Plants Advisory Committee to it. It may well be that it is not too late to stop its spread.

Comment. So, there it is. I think you will agree that, on balance, privet is a bad thing and our policy should be to get rid of it. **How to do that, of course, involves another in-depth discussion**, and I have no doubt that such a discussion will turn up one Christmas sooner or later. So, keep watching for it, and the chance to contribute.

SUMMING UP 1966

Australia in 1966 was a good place to live. There were plenty of jobs, a high standard of living, a reasonable safety net for the disadvantaged, good health and education systems. Whatever you wanted to measure, we were near the top by international standards.

As far as 1966 **events** were concerned, things were also pretty good. We saw the shiny new decimal currency, we proved that the Opera House did not need Utzon to finish it off, and we shook our heads over our cemeteries. The violence of roller games thrilled us, we sorted out where that dog sits, and we tried to get books **into** public libraries. President Johnson did not run over anyone, Mr White got a brand new bride, and Sir Edward got an unwarranted drubbing at the zoo. For the future, we knew we had some problems ahead as Britain left her Empire behind and joined Europe in the Common Market. But, **not to worry, mate, she'll be right.**

All these were matters that came and went. They were all part of the hurly-burly of life, and were to be expected in some form or other.

The one problem for the nation was obviously Vietnam. I do not have to cover that ground again, but let me say that Vietnam was here to stay. I have written many of these books, and generally I have been able **to finish on an upbeat note**. That was **not** true for 1939 to 1942 but after that, even in the War years, **I was able to say that next year would be better.** In the early 1950's, with the Korean War, **that** was a dubious message. But all other years, I could truly say that things had been good, and would be better next year.

Not for **next** year though. Next year, as far as Vietnam is concerned, the situation will deteriorate. The other parts of our lives will be fine. Jobs, the economy, the health system, and so on. Don't forget the Sunday barbie. No problems there. But, try as we may, at the back of all this, every decent Australian will be conscious that in Vietnam more bombs will be dropped, more villages bombed, more forests napalmed, greater atrocities committed, and **more Aussie soldiers and silly young boys will be killed**.

That is the sad picture I have for next year. 50-plus years later, with a lump in my throat, I wish it could be different.

READERS' COMMENTS

Tom Lynch, Speers Point…..Some history writers make the mistake of trying to boost their authority by including graphs and charts all over the place. You on the other hand get a much better effect by saying things like "he made a pile". Or "every one worked hours longer than they should have, and felt like death warmed up at the end of the shift." I have seen other writers waste two pages of statistics painting the same picture as you did in a few words.

Barry Marr, Adelaide….you know that I am being facetious when I say that I wish the war had gone on for years longer so that you would have written more books about it.

Edna College, Auburn….A few times I stopped and sobbed as you brought memories of the postman delivering letters, and the dread that ordinary people felt as he neared. How you captured those feelings yet kept your coverage from becoming maudlin or bogged down is a wonder to me.

Betty Kelly, Wagga Wagga….Every time you seem to be getting serious, you throw in a phrase or memory that lightens up the mood. In particular, in the war when you were describing the terrible carnage of Russian troops, you ended with a ten-line description of how aggrieved you felt and ended it with "apart from that, things are pretty good here". For me, it turned the unbearable into the bearable, and I went from feeling morbid and angry back to a normal human being.

Alan Davey, Brisbane…. I particularly liked the light-hearted way you described the scenes at the airports as American , and British, high-flying entertainers flew in. I had always seen the crowd behavious as disgraceful, but your light-hearted description of it made me realise it was in fact harmless and just good fun.

MORE INFORMATION ON THESE BOOKS

Over the past 16 years the author, Ron Williams, has written this series of books that present a social history of Australia in the post-war period. They cover the period for 1939 to 1972, with one book for each year. Thus there are 34 books.

To capture the material for each book, the author, Ron Williams, worked his way through the *Sydney Morning Herald* and the *Age/Argus* day-by-day, and picked out the best stories, ideas and trivia. He then wrote them up into 180 pages of a year-book.

He writes in a direct conversational style, he has avoided statistics and charts, and has produced easily-read material that is entertaining, and instructive, and charming.

They are invaluable as gifts for birthdays, Christmas, and anniversaries, and for the oldies who are hard to buy for.

These books are available at all major retailers. They are also listed in all the major catalogues, including Title Page, Dymocks and Booktopia.

They can also be ordered through:
www.boombooks.biz
or at jen@boombooks.biz

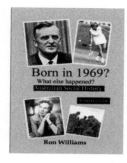

Born in 1969?
What else happened?
Australian Social History

Ron Williams

In 1969. Hollywood produced a fake movie that appeared to show a few Americans walking on the moon. The last stream train was pensioned off as the Indian Pacific crossed the nation. There are now no Labor governments in office in all Australia, but Laborites should not worry because Paul Keating just got a seat in Canberra. Thousands of people walked the streets in demos against the Vietnam War, and HMAS Melbourne cut a US Destroyer in two. The Poseidon nickel boom made the fortunes of many. Oz Magazine died an untimely death.

Born in 1970?
What else happened?
Australian Social History

Ron Williams

In 1970, President Nixon's war in Vietnam, and now Cambodia, was getting unpopular in the USA and Oz. We decided to take our 8th Battalion home. Melbourne's Westgate Bridge fell into the water and killed 35 workmen. The Queen, Prince Phillip, and two kids came to Oz. They liked it, so the Pope came later. Margaret Court, John Newcombe, Shane Gould, and Raylene Boyle all did well overseas, and made us think we were world-beaters. Nick Jagger starred in "Ned Kelly". There were 13 million people and 180 million sheep in Oz.